Virtual Facilitation

Virtual Facilitation

Create More Engagement and Impact

Henrik Horn Andersen
Iben Nelson
Kåre Ronex

WILEY

This edition first published [2021]

© 2021 Implement Consulting Group

Registered office

John Wiley & Sons Ltd, The Atrium, Southern Gate, Chichester, West Sussex, PO19 8SQ, United Kingdom

For details of our global editorial offices, for customer services and for information about how to apply for permission to reuse the copyright material in this book please see our website at www.wiley.com.

Wiley publishes in a variety of print and electronic formats and by print-on-demand. Some material included with standard print versions of this book may not be included in e-books or in print-on-demand. If this book refers to media such as a CD or DVD that is not included in the version you purchased, you may download this material at http://booksupport.wiley.com. For more information about Wiley products, visit www.wiley.com.

Designations used by companies to distinguish their products are often claimed as trademarks. All brand names and product names used in this book are trade names, service marks, trademarks or registered trademarks of their respective owners. The publisher is not associated with any product or vendor mentioned in this book.

Limit of Liability/Disclaimer of Warranty: While the publisher and author have used their best efforts in preparing this book, they make no representations or warranties with respect to the accuracy or completeness of the contents of this book and specifically disclaim any implied warranties of merchantability or fitness for a particular purpose. It is sold on the understanding that the publisher is not engaged in rendering professional services and neither the publisher nor the author shall be liable for damages arising herefrom. If professional advice or other expert assistance is required, the services of a competent professional should be sought.

Library of Congress Cataloging-in-Publication Data

Names: Andersen, Henrik Horn, author. | Nelson, Iben, author. | Ronex, Kare, author.
Title: Virtual facilitation : create more engagement and impact / Henrik Horn Andersen, Iben Nelson, Kare Ronex.
Description: Chichester, West Sussex, United Kingdom : John Wiley & Sons, 2021. | Includes index.
Identifiers: LCCN 2020041520 (print) | LCCN 2020041521 (ebook) | ISBN 9781119765318 (cloth) | ISBN 9781119770572 (adobe pdf) | ISBN 9781119770565 (epub)
Subjects: LCSH: Virtual reality in management. | Group facilitation. | Business meetings. | Virtual work teams. | Employees—Training of—Computer-assisted instruction.
Classification: LCC HD30.2122 .A53 2021 (print) | LCC HD30.2122 (ebook) | DDC 658/.0568--dc23
LC record available at https://lccn.loc.gov/2020041520
LC ebook record available at https://lccn.loc.gov/2020041521

Cover Design: Wiley
Cover Image: Implement Consulting Group
Background: ©Eakachai Leesin/EyeEm/Getty Images

Set in 12/16pt Janson Text LT Std by SPi Global, Chennai, India

Printed and bound by CPI Group (UK) Ltd, Croydon CR0 4YY

10 9 8 7 6 5 4 3 2 1

Contents

Foreword

In March 2020 London Business School, as many other organisations across the world, faced a severe challenge due to the Covid-19 pandemic. A large part of our business (executive education) stopped abruptly, as people were simply unwilling or unable to fly to London. The crisis required us to rethink many fundamental aspects of our business – our view on teaching and learning, on how we collaborate with others, on what exactly people value from a business education – and to do it extremely quickly.

Normally London Business School is a melting pot of bright people, joining MSc and MBA programmes, seeking a state-of-the-art education, and building networks with other like-minded people from all over the world. But in March, with the Covid-19 situation escalating across the world, it was clear that we couldn't deliver on that value proposition in the same way as before.

Our first priority was to ensure that our Masters degree students could continue learning, take the necessary exams, and graduate on the agreed timetable. Which of course meant moving all teaching online. At first, there was scepticism and resistance to this move, but we persevered and it quickly became clear that 'classroom learning' can be recreated quite effectively in Zoom, and sometimes even for the better. Student ratings and exam grades suggest that this wholesale shift to online teaching has been a success.

To be sure, I still have some reservations about online learning. One problem is lower levels of student engagement. My experience in the classroom is around 70% fully engaged and participating in the case study discussions, 20% disengaged (sitting at the back, probably on Facebook) and 10% absent. The comparable numbers for online classes is around 40% engaged, 30% disengaged, 30% absent (and hopefully watching the recording of the class later). So while there is still a decent level of learning achieved by everyone, I think the number who get full value out of the session is much lower. Another challenge is you need a different mindset and focus as a teacher, since you don't get the same quality of feedback from the students. In a classroom setting you often adapt 'in the moment' and you can speed up or slow down, depending on the body language and the questions. But teaching over Zoom you don't get that same quality of insight into what the students are thinking, so there is little scope for deviation.

These reservations aside, online teaching actually works pretty well, at least in terms of building cognitive understanding in the students. But the relational and behavioural parts of learning are much more challenging in a virtual setting – they require more planning and deliberate design, which this book clearly demonstrates and provides inspiration for.

If the teaching part had been the only challenge back in March it wouldn't have been so bad. But of course London Business School is much more than just an educational institution – we also see ourselves as a platform for developing and sharing new business insights on a global basis. So in thinking about ways to make the best of the challenging circumstances, we launched a free live webinar series, initially called 'Leading Through a Pandemic' through to May, and then shifting to 'Beyond the Crisis' from June onwards. In total we had 26 webinars, roughly two per week, on topics ranging from macro-economics through strategy to personal resilience. I hosted the series, and each webinar featured one or two faculty, applying their research insights to the challenges facing businesses in that period of lockdown. The reception was very positive – between 1,500 and 5,000 registered attendees for each webinar, and around 15,000 unique attendees in total. Some were LBS alumni and students, but many were executives who had never interacted with us before, so the PR benefits to the School were huge. To gain additional value out of these webinars, we then pulled them together with some additional pre-recorded materials, readings and assignments, to create an online course 'Building Organisational Resilience' which we made available for purchase even before lockdown was over.

What about the internal challenges of managing the business school during that time? As part of the leadership team, I was putting in long days with back-to-back Zoom calls, trying to tackle all the strategic and operational challenges of reinventing the business for this new, highly uncertain world. And we made our share of mistakes. For example, we were conducting online meetings with the various formal decision-making bodies in the School, and through the usual chains of command, but we did not spend enough time informally socialising our ideas with others outside of these groups. We weren't deliberately keeping people in the dark – but without the short corridor conversations or informal lunches, many people were becoming increasingly frustrated. After a few months we realised that we needed to act differently, and we put in place a series of open sessions for people to join if they could. We established a couple of advisory groups to get input into our redesign of our organisation. Slowly we got the organisation on the same page as the management team and learned a valuable lesson on change management and on virtual collaboration.

It was a rough ride, with a lot of uncertainty, lots of mistakes and learnings along the way but we are now in a much better position with the business and the quality of our offerings and the quality of our virtual sessions. However, I would have appreciated having the input from this book during the process. Luckily there is still a lot to learn for us and a lot of practical tools and ideas in the following pages that we have yet to use. Our ambition is to keep on learning and developing our service on this area in the years to come.

Enjoy reading!

—Julian Birkinshaw
Professor and Deputy Dean, London Business School

Introduction

How often have you been in a virtual meeting and felt as though it was all about one-way communication? Have you found yourself wondering why the person running the meeting couldn't have just sent you an email or a screen recording? Do you find yourself reaching for your phone or checking your emails so you can 'multitask'? Do you make affirmative noises just so it looks as though you're listening? Do you wonder how engaged the other participants are? Our research shows that 60% of participants do other work-related tasks and 47% even have tried to go to the toilet during a virtual meeting!

If you can relate to this scenario you're certainly not alone. We've all been there – and not only in virtual meetings, although virtual meetings have now gained a new level of importance. The Covid-19 pandemic definitely accelerated the use of virtual technology within business. However, the trend towards virtual working had already emerged prior to 2020. In fact, its popularity has been rising for several years.

Firstly, the climate crisis has encouraged, and in some cases even forced, companies to evaluate their carbon footprint and explore more environmentally friendly and sustainable ways of doing business. It's clear that changing global business practices will be vital in helping fight the climate crisis. Turning to virtual sessions that require less travel and therefore generate less pollution, as well as bringing teams from around the world together, will be essential if we are to have a positive impact on the planet for future generations.

Secondly, we live in an increasingly globalised world. Collaborating across physical boundaries has never been more relevant. Businesses can have employees based all over the world, or work with partner organisations around the globe. Communicating and collaborating in a virtual environment has become more important than ever.

Thirdly, there are cost benefits to virtual working. Businesses can reduce the amount they spend on travel.

Finally, virtual working allows organisations to tap into expertise that may not otherwise be easily accessible to them.

Virtual working is all about speeding up processes and bringing the right people together at the right time. In this book we will zoom in on virtual facilitation as an important part of virtual work.

What is virtual facilitation?

In its purest form, facilitation is about helping a group perform better, whether that's helping them reach an outcome more quickly, more efficiently or even going further than they thought possible. We take this concept of facilitation, of improving the process, and bring it to the virtual world.

The Covid-19 pandemic has accelerated the shift to working in a virtual space. There's also pressure for businesses to be more efficient, which is adding to the need to work in virtual environments. But what we've noticed is that, while many businesses are embracing these virtual opportunities, many also lack the skills, knowledge or insight to get the most out of them. The sudden need to adapt working practices to virtual environments means that there has been a steep learning curve, and many are finding it difficult to realise the full potential of their virtual meetings.

We have heard people saying that they feel as though they're losing momentum in their business, that they're seeing employee engagement fall, and that there is a lack of energy within the company. Businesses are aware that there are problems, but they don't know how to address them effectively in this new, predominantly virtual world. On the other hand, we have also seen very effective meetings, high productivity while working from home and employees that value the flexibility of virtual meetings.

Throughout this book we will share our extensive knowledge on virtual facilitation, based on a wealth of practical experience that provides you with the tools we use ourselves: to ensure high-quality sessions, ideas and inspiration on how to get more out of your virtual meetings, workshops and training.

When you facilitate a meeting effectively, you'll see a number of benefits. Attendees will be actively engaged and contributing to the meeting or workshop, rather than just being 'present'. People will be more motivated, they'll take ownership of the decisions made in the meeting and there will be a more positive energy, both in the meeting and beyond. All of these elements will have a positive impact in terms of what happens after the meeting.

For employers, this is an opportunity to create a real buzz in your organisation and to make employees feel valued. We all know that people leave jobs because they feel undervalued by their manager. If you're increasingly working in a virtual environment, you need to make sure that your employees know they're valued and are able to contribute in that virtual space.

This is about future-proofing your organisation. Businesses don't just need their employees to put the hours in. Efficiency isn't enough any longer. The winning formula that you need for future success will involve being efficient, but it will also require you to tap into the creativity, engagement and motivation of your employees.

The advantages of virtual facilitation

There are many advantages to virtual facilitation, which we'll explore in greater detail as we move through the book. They include:

- The ability to bring the right people together.
- The opportunity to introduce experts.
- Making training more accessible.
- Providing more frequent touchpoints.
- Enabling more effective sessions.
- Better data access during sessions.
- Easier documentation of the process and outcomes.
- More equal contributions from all participants.

Putting the human back into the digital world

We're not advocating for entirely digital workplaces. We understand that, for many people, going to work is as much about the social interaction with colleagues and clients as it is about doing a specific job. But there is no need to choose between the physical or the virtual. You can have both.

Our aim is to help people to have more meaningful interactions. We want to help businesses understand how virtual spaces can also be social, without making a meeting less efficient or productive. There are many benefits to operating in a virtual world, but there is still a place for physical meetings and events. Based on your knowledge of physical and virtual sessions you should decide when the situation calls for a physical or a virtual meeting. Our approach is about making sure that when we are together, we're together in a more meaningful way

Humans are social creatures who need to connect and build relationships on a personal level. In the following pages, we'll not only cover the positive business impact of a good virtual meeting, but also the positive people impact of a good virtual meeting.

Our aim is to share our knowledge and expertise to help you create a productive and engaging meeting culture at your organisation, where you take full advantage of the virtual space in your ongoing collaborations. We want to put a human element into the digital world.

Sharing the 'How'

We want to use our knowledge, skills and understanding of virtual facilitation to help businesses of all sizes, and across all industries, to raise the quality of their virtual sessions. Our purpose is to help you and your teams to spend your time more wisely and create an even greater impact.

Through this book, we want to help you make sense of the virtual world. We're not just going to talk about the technical aspects of virtual facilitation – we're bringing our years of experience in human behaviour to combine humans with the technical possibilities that lie before us.

This book is a practical guide to facilitating effective and engaging virtual sessions – from practitioners to practitioners. From January to May 2020 in our company, Implement Consulting Group, we hosted 33,731 Teams sessions with internal or external participants, been part of 4,152 Zoom sessions either as facilitators or participants and hosted 161 Zoom Webinars with a total number of 62,634 people attending these Zoom meetings.

Based on our extensive experience facilitating small and large virtual events for companies across the globe, hosting webinars and training of more people in virtual facilitation this book reveals what really works. We'll share small and easy steps that you can take at every stage, helping you to change the world, one session at a time. Most of the solutions we present in this book are scalable. They work for sessions involving 5 people, 50 people and even 500 people.

With our practical tools you can have a positive impact on virtual sessions immediately, whether you're responsible for facilitating large or small virtual sessions. These are some of the questions you'll find answers to:

- How do I plan virtual sessions with impact and engagement?
- How do I engage people in a virtual session?
- How can I get my message across and connect with many people in different places?
- How can I use virtual facilitation to drive change at my organisation?

We want to open your eyes to what is possible with today's virtual technology and to show you where opportunities lie for your business. As we have said before, this book isn't just about what is possible, but about how you can get there. This book is designed to be one that you can dip in and out of as you need to, where you can find practical advice about facilitating virtual meetings, workshops and other events as well as tools that you can use to improve the quality of your virtual sessions immediately and create value for you and your business.

A blend of expertise

Henrik is one of the best facilitators in Denmark. He started his career conducting analysis and producing reports to inform organisational change. However, he quickly realised that strategic analysis alone isn't enough to deliver meaningful change. He started exploring how to engage organisations with the strategies he was developing, which resulted in him conducting a substantial number of workshops, and training others in facilitation. He has worked at Implement Consulting Group for 16 years and has also co-authored the book *Facilitation – Create Results Through Involvement* with Cecilie van Loon and Line Larsen, which was published in both Danish and English.

Iben is a learning expert. She specialises in the field of learning and facilitation, training internal consultants as well as clients. She has extensive experience within facilitation, designing and executing leadership training, workshops, and larger events, as well as a passion for helping professionals learn and grow. She enjoys the challenge of a steep learning curve and takes a practical approach to learning, whether she's working with MBA students, Implement consultants or corporate clients. She is currently exploring how new workspaces will look as the virtual and the physical environments are combined.

Kåre is a qualified school teacher with a Master's degree in Positive Psychology. For many years, his focus was on not only achieving the learning objectives he needed to with his students, but on ensuring that what he was teaching them stuck. How to make learning stick, how to spend time wisely and how to get the most out of time spent together are questions that he's spent years focusing on. His combined knowledge of technology, psychology and facilitation make his approach to virtual facilitation unique and led him to Implement Consulting Group.

Although we are all on different journeys, we share the belief that everyone can learn to host better meetings, if they understand the dynamics and have effective tools at their disposal. Our work at Implement Consulting Group is just that: implementing tools and techniques to have a positive impact and deliver meaningful change within an organisation.

What unites us across our various disciplines is that we have a passion for driving change, but we also bring a human perspective to our work. In this book, we'll share examples and case studies relating to everything from the supply chain and sales projects to digital and commercial transformations. We're sharing the knowledge that we have among our 900 consulting staff with you in this book.

For two years running, Implement Consulting Group has been named as having the best consultancy company culture in Europe. We have consistently outgrown the market and work with our global network of trainers and consultants to help businesses all over the world improve the quality of their virtual meetings, workshops and events.

In April and May 2020 alone, we hosted over 45 unique webinars and trained more than 5,000 people in virtual facilitation.

Diving into the digital world

We've broken the book up into five parts. In Part I we'll explore the core of virtual sessions and how to facilitate them.

Part II covers the preparation before your virtual session, including how to design and plan high-quality meetings. In Part III we explain what to do during a good virtual session, providing useful tools and techniques that you can introduce to keep everyone engaged. Part IV is all about what you do after your virtual session, including how you evaluate a session, collect feedback and follow up with participants.

In Part V, we'll delve into specific workshop and meeting formats to give you additional tools to use in certain scenarios, and practical advice to help you facilitate better meetings.

Throughout the book we'll provide you with examples to inspire you and show you how the tools and techniques we share can have a positive impact.

We have designed this book to be a guide that you can return to time and again. Don't expect to implement everything we discuss immediately. What we hope you'll do is to get inspired, introduce one or two techniques initially and, once you master those, return to the book to broaden your knowledge further and find new areas where you can develop your skills in facilitating virtual sessions.

Use our online platform to get materials and the newest inspiration

We have deliberately focused on general methods, tools and techniques for facilitating the human element of virtual sessions. We aren't offering a comprehensive insight into the available technology, because that would likely mean the book would be out of date before it was even published. Instead we have made an online platform for the book. You can find it here: www.implement.dk/virtual-facilitation.

We have already placed some items online to accompany this book, such as the templates we describe alongside some useful material for process methods. You'll find links throughout the book directing you to these relevant resources and materials. We have also provided extra content such as inspirational blog posts about the software we use. You can get in touch through the site, and we will continue to share news within the field of virtual facilitation and hope you'll use this resource actively.

Create a personal training program for you as a virtual facilitator

This book is designed to accompany your development. We want to provide practical advice that will have an impact and help you improve the quality of your meetings, both virtual and in real life.

There is a world of opportunities waiting for you. If you go into this space with an open mind, what we're about to share with you can have a significant impact and generate a great deal of positive energy. We want to open up the world to you and your organisation. There are many people working in a virtual environment at the moment, but very few have mastered it. We're here to help you take the right steps towards mastering virtual facilitation.

A very practical suggestion to help you grow and learn as a virtual facilitator is to take notes as you read through the book. Mark the things you think would benefit your sessions and note what and where. It could be on a piece of paper, using Post-it notes or with dog ears and a small note in the margin.

After you finish the book, your notes can help you to review the things that really inspired you or were specially useful for you. That way you have your own little virtual facilitation program, right at hand. Ready to train, test and learn from. Start with the most important thing, experiment, get feedback and learn to master it before you move on to the next thing.

Good luck reading, training and facilitating.

Happy reading!

I

The Core of Virtual Facilitation

In this first part of the book, we're going to dig into the basics of the good virtual session, whether it is a meeting, a workshop or training, explain what virtual facilitation is, and how it can result in a good virtual session. This is about cultivating the right mindset for your virtual sessions, and understanding the essentials – including how to set the scene for the session, what it means to go virtual, what a virtual facilitator actually is and preparing yourself with the right technological setup.

1

An Introduction to Facilitating Sessions

L et's begin by defining what we mean when we talk about facilitation. The word itself comes from the Latin word *facilis*, which means to make something easier or to move freely. This is the first of several ways of looking at facilitation, which are all interconnected. As well as making things easier and free flowing, facilitation can be described as the process of channeling the energy and communication of a group working on a particular matter to deliver a better outcome than if they were working on their own. At its core, it's about helping groups to do better. A facilitator is a person doing the facilitation.

Facilitation is a way to create ownership and impact by involving participants at the right level. The aim is to ensure that, in each session, we move forward with whatever tasks we're discussing. Virtual facilitation is very much built upon traditional facilitation. Many of the tools you would use in a physical meeting still apply – you simply need to transfer them to a virtual environment.

In this chapter we'll cover several models, including:

- The Five Levels of Involvement: When do you need to tell? When you need to sell? When do you need to test? When do you need to consult? When do you need to co-create?
- The Corner Flags model: Once you know the context of your meeting and how you want to involve people, you need to be very specific and transparent about what you will and won't discuss. You're defining what is inside the corner flags and what is outside of them.

What is a good virtual meeting?

As we mentioned in the Introduction to the book, a good meeting is one where we are focused on the result and where we are involving participants at the right level. That means we're bringing in the participants that we need and starting with a firm purpose. Having a clear purpose is essential as this defines why you need to spend time on something and ensures that, during your meeting, you achieve it.

We believe a good meeting should also create ownership and involvement among the participants. If you need your participants to contribute to the creation of impact and solutions after the meeting, you want them to be engaged and to follow along and possibly even contribute in the future. A good meeting will move people in the direction that you want to go in and get them involved in the project or task.

Virtual interactions always need a facilitator

In a virtual space, it's even more important to have a facilitator than in a physical meeting. When participants aren't in the same physical space, they often hold back and it can be harder to get everyone to work together. You need someone who can make it easy to participate – someone who will pass the 'ball', tell people when it's their turn to contribute and then bring the 'ball' back and pass it to the next person. It's important to have a facilitator to prompt the participants to offer their opinions. A facilitator is essential to good meetings in the virtual space.

What happens when there is no facilitator?

How often have you finished a meeting or session and then heard phrases like:

- 'It was so hard for us to settle on something concrete.'
- 'It was really hard to reach the target.'
- 'I'm not sure what we actually decided in the meeting.'

These, and similar phrases, are a strong sign that there was no facilitator in that session. That means these sessions aren't as effective or useful as they could be.

It's important to own the role of facilitator. Before every session you could ask the question: 'Who will facilitate this session?' This helps to cultivate the mindset of having someone who owns that process.

What does your meeting culture look like?

Every business has a virtual meeting culture. This culture could be that they never make decisions in meetings but just log into a virtual space, discuss things and see what comes out of it. The culture can also be defined by the types of meetings you have. They might always be one-way communication from the organiser, uncontrolled group discussions, or involve jamming on a virtual whiteboard with no real follow-up or impact afterwards. However, by using the right kind of meetings at the right time, with a clear purpose and follow-ups to ensure impact and effect, this meeting culture can look very different.

In many large organisations, you could describe the meeting culture as one where people aren't engaged. People arrive late, they aren't prepared, no agenda is set or sent out in advance, and people don't use their camera.

For us, a good virtual meeting culture is one where the participants and facilitator are prepared for the meetings they go to, have thought about what will be discussed and why the session is taking place, with all participants actively involved in the meeting. Also it's about planning for before, during and after to ensure impact. And it's about having the technical requirements in place using video with good lighting and proper sound. Finally, it's about keeping people engaged to ensure ownership and action afterwards.

Don't wait for the entire culture at your organisation to change. You can start with your own sessions and make sure they are well run so that you're getting the most out of the meetings that you facilitate and attend. In terms of physical meetings, many organisations already have a settled meeting culture. However, this is different in the virtual space. This meeting culture is still emerging and has yet to be defined. This presents an opportunity for you to shape it into a valuable one, where you avoid the pitfalls and create good virtual meetings.

Why have meetings?

As a facilitator, or host, you should only have a meeting if there's something to discuss. As a participant, have you ever tried to decline a meeting because it didn't make sense for you? There should be a real reason to gather people, namely to create an impact or change. This impact and change should continue beyond the meeting. Our approach is very much about creating impact and change through ownership and involvement, in order to create understanding, acceptance and behavioural change to move an organisation in a certain direction. This approach means it is your job as a facilitator to make your meetings relevant for your participants. Sending an Outlook invitation with a link to the session isn't enough.

The difference between a meeting, a workshop and training

We're not only going to talk about facilitating virtual meetings in this book, but all kinds of virtual sessions. It's therefore important to understand the difference between a meeting, a workshop and a training session. As a broad term for all we will use the term 'session'.

A meeting is often something that reoccurs. It might be a weekly departmental status meeting, for example, or a regular update meeting within your organisation. Meetings are often focused on knowledge sharing, planning or sharing the status of progress.

A workshop will usually be more interactive. You'll use workshops when you're at the start of a process, where you need more input from participants or where you're creating something new or generating ideas. They can be small (from five participants) to large (1,000 participants).

A training session is usually focused on building up the participants' knowledge from a trainer and giving them opportunities to apply it through exercises, as well as to receive feedback on their progress.

Of course, elements from meetings can be part of workshops or training, and vice versa. Most tools we'll explore later in the book can be applied in any virtual setting.

The Five Levels of Involvement

When we plan at a session, one starting point is how we want the participants to contribute (Figure 1.1). Do we need to involve our participants to a lesser or greater degree to reach our goal? This affects the participant's ownership to the solution as well as the facilitator's control over the content.

Telling is where you have greatest control over the content and the solution. As you climb that ladder, you as the facilitator have less control. But what you lose in control you gain in ownership of the solution among other people at your organisation. The higher the level of involvement in reaching a solution, the higher the level of ownership because people feel part of the solution.

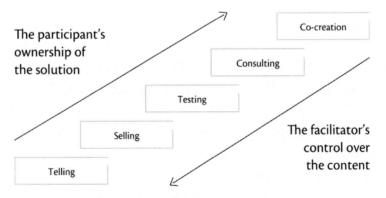

Figure 1.1   The Five Levels of Involvement

When to use the different levels of involvement?

- Tell: This would most commonly be applied in an information meeting. For example, if there is going to be a big change in your company and you want to tell your employees about it, you will inform them. Employees aren't going to be highly involved. You might ask a question at the end, but the main purpose is to share important information and typically that would be in a meeting format, rather than a workshop. You might have a telling element to a workshop where you set the scene and put the purpose in context, but this wouldn't comprise the majority of the workshop.

- Sell: When you're selling you have a preferred solution in mind and want to engage in dialogue around that solution. You're not just telling everyone what the solution is and dictating how things will go, but you do have a solution to discuss. This might take the format of a Q&A session, where you're able to dig deeper into the concerns and challenges surrounding the solution. But you're not talking about changing the solution, you're exploring that solution. Similar to telling, you might have a selling element at the beginning of a workshop, but it won't comprise the whole session. Selling is more likely in a meeting.

- Test: When you're testing something, you're approaching it from the perspective that you have a solution that's 90% there, but you want to make sure you get it to 100% in terms of quality or efficiency or whatever. You're seeking input to improve the solution, but again not to change it fundamentally. Testing is more likely in a meeting, but could also be in a workshop.

- Consult: Consulting is where you have two (or maybe more) options and are asking for help to decide which is the right one to choose. At this stage you're moving away from

Telling	Selling	Testing	Training	Co-creating
– PowerPoint presentation.	– Q&A session.	– Survey.	– Sharing information and letting people work with it themselves.	– Crazy Eights (Google Sprint method).
– Interviewing a key stakeholder where you're sharing the same information but in a different format.	– Reflective exercises where you talk about why something makes sense.	– Where is the mood?		– Whiteboard exercises.
		– Which one solution do you see working?	– Breakout rooms.	
		– Mentimeter.	– Tasks.	– Idea generation work.
	– Structured processes that look at strengths or opportunities.	– Polling exercises.	– Connecting information to their own world.	– Miro.
		– Double bookkeeping.		
		– Future scenarios: How will this look in two years?	– As the facilitator, you decide on how interactive it will be.	– Digital Post-it exercises.

a meeting and towards a workshop, because you require a much greater level of participation from those attending.

- Co-create: Co-creating is where you're asking for help to find a solution. You have a problem and a blank piece of paper and you're looking for a solution or idea to solve that problem. This will usually take the format of a workshop rather than a meeting.

There is an important distinction between control of the content and control of the process. Releasing control of the content doesn't mean you release control of the process. For example, at co-creation, you can let go of control of the content or solution, while maintaining a high degree of control of the process.

For example, you could say: 'You have 20 minutes to come up with four ideas. They need to be in this format or template. What the ideas are is up to you, but you need to come back with four ideas in 20 minutes.' Here, you're completely releasing control of the content, but you're keeping very tight control of the process.

Put your session into context

Before you start designing your session, you need to understand the context of the situation. If you are external, you also want to find out the strategy and direction of the organisation. If you're part of the organisation you'll probably already have an understanding of this. But look at how this project, or this session or part of the project, fits into a wider strategy. Are there interdependencies with other projects? Are there other things coming down the line that will affect it? Are there parallel work streams you need to be aware of? Putting your session in this context is important before you start to design it.

Ask the following questions:

- What is the big journey that this meeting taps into?
- What impact is this meeting going to support?

Next you move into the Corner Flags model (Figure 1.2). The Corner Flags model is a tool to help you qualify the boundaries of your session and help you be clear in your communication and deliberate in your involvement.

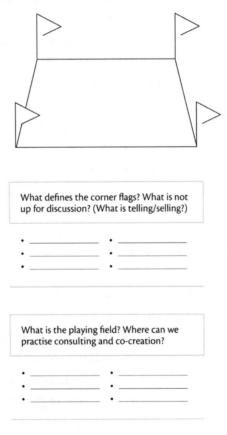

What defines the corner flags? What is not up for discussion? (What is telling/selling?)

- _____   - _____
- _____   - _____
- _____   - _____

What is the playing field? Where can we practise consulting and co-creation?

- _____   - _____
- _____   - _____
- _____   - _____

Figure 1.2   The Corner Flags model

The Corner Flags model is a mental picture and a tool to ensure that you, as the facilitator, define what the playing field for your session looks like, design for it and help your players – the participants – to play the right game and add value where it makes sense.

Sometimes participants prefer to go outside the corner flags as they are engaged or have an opinion on something that is outside of the playing field. To avoid misunderstandings and lower engagement it is important to be clear about where you can and can't affect the decisions and thereby avoid derailing the purpose of the session. Defining and communicating the corner flags at the start of the session helps you as a facilitator to get them back on track if the discussion gets sidetracked – it's simply easier to say 'this is not within the scope of this session, would it be okay to park it here and address it another time?' If you do not set the corner flags from the start, it can be much harder to get them to focus on the field.

The Corner Flag model is key to make your players – the participants – play the game, not waste their time running around outside the field.

When you look at the session ask yourself, 'What defines the corner flags of this session?' These are the elements not up for discussion – the parts where you tell or sell. The board might have given you the task of developing a new product for a specific target group. That target group, along with the development of a new product, would be two corners of the playing field that are not up for discussion.

Ask yourself the following questions to define your corner flags:

- 'What defines the corner flags of this session?'
- 'What is settled?'
- 'What is up for discussion?'

Next, take a deeper look at the playing field. What does it look like? What do you want your participants to discuss or contribute with? Where do they have a say? How much of a say do they have? People get motivated by autonomy, among other things, so make sure you create a field for them to play in. A place where they are consulted and can co-create. Even if it is small, make it visible.

In a soccer field there would be four corner flags. You don't need to have this – your field can look different. It can be small or large. Sometimes you play on a big field where people have a lot to say. Other times the field is smaller. It's your role as facilitator to make sure it's there. Set the flags and define the playing field.

Make sure you're clear, to all participants, what has already been decided, what is not up for discussion and what you actually need to discuss at this point in the project.

How-to guide: The Corner Flags model

To help you be clear – where the participants can be genuinely involved and where there have already been decisions made – we suggest that you use this template, either in your own preparation or in your discussions with the customer/ manager. The aim here is to help you become clearer in your communication and more aware of which levels of involvement to go for.

1. Start by brainstorming what has already been decided with regards to the topic (i.e. the project) and what is not up for discussion in the session, given the purpose and the group of people assembled.

2. Then fill in the second part, focusing on where you are really interested in collecting input and where there is room for discussion and adjustments.

3. Use this input in your preparation of materials and scripts and in communication, up to and on the actual day, to create clarity and avoid pseudo-involvement.

The meeting itself won't create a business-wide impact or behavioural change, but it is part of the process of gathering new insights and producing new results and ideas that can tap into this bigger journey.

Start working on your virtual sessions

There are four elements of a good meeting and we'll discuss each in turn throughout this book. The first element is zooming out and getting the big picture. You need to understand the context of your meeting or session. The Corner Flags model can be used for inspiration here. From there you move into the elements that are detailed in Parts II, III and IV of this book: before, during and after.

Before the session you will design it using the Design Star and the Script, do the practical preparations and invite and prepare your participants. During the session you will execute the plan and, after the session, you will get feedback and follow up. Any good meeting will have these four elements.

Many people are confident in their ability to plan and run physical meetings, but they find themselves in a different situation and feeling less confident when they are running sessions in a virtual environment. It's a new ball game, so to speak, and you need to brush up on the rules. That's why it's so important to do your homework and not simply assume that you can run a virtual session in the same way that you'd run a physical one.

Now that you have an overview of what's required to have a high-quality session, both in a physical and virtual environment, it's time to explore how to create high-quality virtual sessions in more detail.

2

Going Virtual with Your Session

We are entering a new space – a space with new opportunities and limitations. In fact, as we write this book, many more people are starting to use technology and the virtual space as a result of increased home working during the Covid-19 pandemic. Many people may find themselves getting new competencies, yet feeling a little uncomfortable, as this new virtual space takes them out of their comfort zone and brings them to an area where they are likely to need a bit of guidance to understand what can be achieved here. We want to help people understand this new space and how to transition from a physical world into a virtual world.

Many of the thoughts around facilitation in a physical setting, in terms of how we engage people and proceed, still apply, although some things are different. However, we often notice that when people are put in a virtual environment, they think that what they know about how to engage and run meetings in person doesn't apply here. Our experience and the perspective of this chapter is that a lot of what you already know can and does still apply. Having said that, there are also new opportunities to create value in a virtual setting.

The definition of virtual that we use is 'not physically existing as such, but made by software to appear to do so'. Our bodies are bound by the physical space, but we can create a virtual space where we meet, work and create impact together.

We believe that the discipline of virtual facilitation has great potential if we look at all of the technological options in the virtual space through the lens of humans and their psychology. Using the virtual space to drive processes can be highly effective, when it's used correctly. Realising this potential requires an effort for facilitators and participants. Within your organisation, you may need to develop new skills to leverage the full potential of the virtual opportunities.

We forget the essentials

A good virtual meeting is different to a physical one due to the simple fact that we meet in a virtual space that gives us different opportunities for collaboration and facilitation. However, the approach to good virtual meetings is very close to the approach to good physical meetings. What we recommend you do when you go into a virtual meeting is continue to think of all the elements you'd consider for a face-to-face meeting. For example, if you were organising a physical meeting you'd ask questions like:

- Why do we meet?
- How will we be meeting up?
- What will I do with the people in the meeting?
- How will I make sure people are comfortable?
- What will I do to make sure people are prepared and have everything they need?

Often in virtual settings, we see people forgetting all of these elements. It's a case of logging in, going through the slides and that's it. They forget to think about the whole journey. In a face-to-face meeting you'd prepare the meeting room, you'd make sure there was coffee available, you'd have someone to greet the attendees as they arrived, you'd make small talk and be really clear about your agenda.

How do people behave in virtual meetings?

Research[1] shows that professionals expect to spend 26% of their time in meetings. However, when we're in virtual meetings we behave in a way that we wouldn't if we were in a face-to-face setting. For example, 65% of people admitted that they carried out other work-related tasks while in a virtual meeting, 47% even went to the toilet, and 50% were eating or cooking during a virtual meeting (Figure 2.1).

This indicates that people don't feel engaged in virtual meetings. It also shows that many virtual meetings aren't efficient at the moment because people aren't fully present. We know that the brain cannot multitask, which means if people are working, emailing or cooking during a virtual meeting then they're not being efficient with their time.

To change this pattern of behaviour, you as a facilitator need to engage people in the meeting, show them that the meeting is meaningful, and make them feel responsible for their presence and attention. The reason why people behave like this isn't because they're stupid, it's because they don't feel the need to be in that meeting and probably with good reason. The other reason they do things like take a toilet break or cook is because they don't think anyone will notice if they're not there.

[1]https://www.westuc.com/en-us/blog/conferencing-collaboration/top-pains-and-potential-video-conferencing

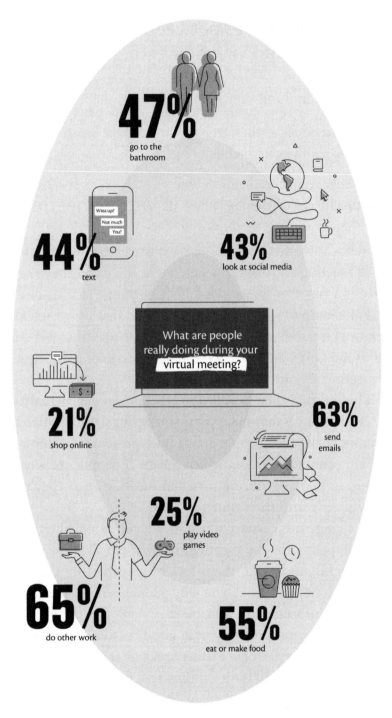

Figure 2.1   How people behave in virtual meetings

Similarities between physical and virtual meetings

One of the main things that physical and virtual meetings should have in common is a really clear purpose as to why people are attending. Everyone who's in the meeting needs to know why they're there and what role they will play. They should also know how to engage in the meeting and what the corner flags are, as we discussed in the previous chapter.

When you're in the design and planning process, you will look at the purpose, the participants, the platform, process and partners. In that sense the structure around designing your meeting is the same whether you're planning a face-to-face or virtual meeting. Many of the tricks that we use during the session as facilitators will also be the same. We will simply need to tweak them to make them work on a virtual platform.

How are virtual meetings different?

There are other constraints in a virtual world though. One thing is the distance (covered later in this chapter), but also that it can be more difficult being flexible and being able to get immediate feedback from the people in the session. You can't just scan the room and see everyone's body language when you're running a virtual session, for instance. Also it can be more difficult to deliver an exercise on the fly in a virtual environment than in a physical one, as templates, instructions etc. need to be prepared in advance.

Therefore, you need to design your process to be a little more firm in a virtual environment. You also need to spend more time planning a good virtual workshop or meeting than one that you'll be delivering face-to-face. However, where you spend more time in planning a virtual meeting, you'll spend less time during the session and on the follow-up activities.

In virtual meetings, all the participants will be contributing digitally. You may use collaborative documents or other similar tools. That means that, with good preparation, everything that happens in the session, all the input, is already documented in one place and ready to share. In face-to-face meetings you might have Post-it notes, flipcharts and other physical notes that you need to sit down and collate once the session finishes. With virtual sessions we would advise you to front-load your time, more so than with face-to-face meetings.

Virtual meetings also tend to be planned more strictly and are therefore more efficient. We're able to be more productive because we don't lose time in the same way that we do in face-to-face meetings. For instance, we might lose ten minutes sending people on a breakout session and another ten minutes getting them back. In virtual meetings, we save those 20 minutes and that allows us to be more productive in a shorter period of time.

Understanding the advantages of virtual facilitation

In our experience, people often aren't fully aware of the advantages that virtual meetings and workshops offer. But there are many benefits to running sessions in a virtual environment.

Bringing the right people together

One of the biggest advantages is the ability to bring the right people into a project using fewer resources. From a climate perspective, it means much less travel, which obviously has a positive impact on the carbon footprint of a business. From a business perspective, it ensures that you always have the strongest possible team working on a project.

Introduce experts

When you run sessions virtually it's also much easier to bring in experts. Virtual sessions can give you access to experts from around the world, without the associated cost, logistics or time of international travel. This can open up many more opportunities, both to your business and your team, in terms of the training and expertise they can access.

Make training more accessible

People have a wide range of training opportunities, but these are often only made available locally. That means, if you're in different offices, it's actually harder for you to attend these training sessions due to the time and travel expenses involved. Imagine that your training was made more broadly available across the organisation and everyone was able to attend it. In doing this you make it much more accessible.

More frequent touchpoints

Changing people's behaviour and understanding is not a one-time thing. We know that frequent refreshers are crucial for real change. Short virtual touchpoints can make this much easier and more efficient than gathering everyone together in the same place physically. For instance, if you want to follow up on something, it's much easier to do so virtually and thereby reduce travel time. We also know that in terms of learning and transfer of knowledge and skills, humans need more than just a one-off session. We have a learning curve and also a forgetting curve. You can fight that forgetting curve with multiple touch-points. These don't need to be long sessions, but they need to be frequent. The virtual space more easily allows us to have these shorter, more frequent touchpoints to reinforce learning and skills development.

More effective sessions

As we've already mentioned, you'll typically spend more time planning a virtual session than one that takes place face-to-face, but this results in more effective meetings. For instance, as facilitators what we would maybe have spent a full day on if we were running a session face-to-face can be condensed into four hours and still deliver the same level of output, provided the meeting is prepared in the right way.

Better data access during a session

As a facilitator, virtual sessions provide you with an opportunity to receive almost instant input from all the participants. This brings you data during a session that you can use to steer the direction and delivery of that session. Think about how much more easily you can engage your whole organisation virtually rather than physically.

Easier documentation of the process and outcomes

As we've already mentioned, in virtual meetings you'll often be working on collaborative documents. That means that at the end of the session all of the output is already recorded and is usually in a format that is ready to share. In many cases, it's easier to get everyone to contribute and be involved in the process when you're in a virtual environment. There's also no danger that a

Post-it note will get misplaced or thrown away before its content has been recorded. It's all there in the virtual space.

More equal contributions from everyone

In a physical space, some people can be very present with their body language and energy and this can allow them to dominate the session. In a virtual environment that's not possible. Everyone is more equal, and that means it can be easier to engage everyone and therefore get a more uniform contribution from all the participants.

The four barriers in virtual meetings

There are four main barriers in virtual meetings that you should be aware of and handle in your sessions (Figure 2.2):

| Physical | Social | Cultural | Technological |
| distance | distance | distance | distance |

Figure 2.2   The four main barriers in virtual meetings

- Physical distance
- Social distance
- Cultural distance
- Technological distance

While these can be barriers to good virtual sessions, there are solutions to each of them that we'll share with you now.

Physical distance

It's obvious that, during a virtual session, we won't be in the same room and therefore, as a facilitator, you're unable to take care of the surroundings. You're not able to ensure that there are no distractions for each participant, that they've closed their door, and so on. You can't make sure that each person has coffee, water or access to the toilet, or that they all have a pen and paper in front of them. And you don't have the informal social contract of being present together to create focus on the session. As the facilitator, you have no direct control over these things. Similarly, you're not able to see from people's body language whether they're following you and engaging. When you are physically in a room with all the participants, you read that room. You can see people nodding and smiling. It can therefore be difficult to judge how everyone is receiving your session. If you've never met some of the participants in person, it can be difficult to judge what type of person they are, whether they're an introvert or extrovert for instance.

Solutions

There are several things you can do to help overcome these physical barriers:

1. Get all the participants to meet physically beforehand or at the start of the project. As the facilitator, that allows you to see who the introverts and extroverts in the group are. You can see how everyone is behaving, and later when you're delivering virtual sessions you will be able to visualise that and design your sessions accordingly.
2. When you're running virtual meetings, it's your responsibility to make sure that everyone sits down in the right physical

setting. Make it part of your role to check that everyone has a coffee or water at the start of the session, and that they have a pen and paper to hand if they'll need those things.

3. Be clear on what everyone needs to do to prepare for the session and what they will need.
4. Consider how you'll handle meetings across different time zones. Sometimes it can make sense to split meetings into two time zones: either Eastern or Western.
5. Turn your webcam on and make sure that everyone else does the same. That can help you to read body language and see how people are responding.

Social distance

In a virtual setting, people tend to find it more difficult to connect with one another. This can make it challenging to build intimacy and trust and for people to feel as though they're part of a team. Often in virtual sessions you see the facilitator going straight to the agenda and getting started without any 'chit-chat'. There's none of the informal conversation at the coffee machine in the ten minutes before the meeting starts where you can ask one another, 'How's life?' But connecting in this informal way is essential for creating trust and a sense of being part of a team.

Solutions

There are several things you can do to overcome these social barriers:

1. Start the meeting five minutes early to ask informal questions and enable that chat. Ask things like, 'How are you doing?' and 'Where are you calling from?'

2. Use breakout rooms, and split into smaller groups of no more than five participants, as much as possible. We often notice that when there are more than four or five people in a room, most people tend to go quiet and don't engage in plenary discussion. Often that's because they don't want to disturb other people, rather than due to a lack of trust, so people will typically be more open and talkative in smaller groups.

3. Facilitate breaks, and make sure that you plan time for these in your session. This is about more than giving people five minutes to get a coffee and go to the bathroom. Allow some time for informal chat during these breaks too.

4. Check the energy levels at the beginning of the meeting and start by getting everybody to do something together. That might be physically moving our bodies or just having a little bit of fun. You might tie this into the informal chat by asking a question like, 'What's the best thing that happened to you this weekend?' and giving everyone time to share that.

5. Get everyone to turn on their videos. We understand that, especially when you're working from home, you may prefer to have your video off, but it's important for everyone's engagement that you use video as much as possible. Encourage people to blur the background if they would prefer to do so. Make sure that people know how to hide the view of themselves but still see the other participants. For some people, being able to see themselves on screen can be distracting, so share options to allow people to use their video without having to see themselves. Turning on the video will also encourage everyone to be engaged. They are much less likely to start multitasking and doing other things during a meeting if their video is switched on.

Cultural distance

Cultural distance has to do with being aware that, when you're working with people from around the world, there may not be the same alignment in terms of how you run meetings or how people behave in meetings. Absorbing these different cultures can be challenging in a virtual space. If you were to fly to China now from Europe, you would feel the culture as you arrived and stayed in the country and you'd probably align a little bit, possibly without even realising it. In virtual meetings there can be a clash of cultures no one realises. Some people might just sit back and not know how to be a part of the meeting as the way the meeting is run is new and different to them. Others might raise their hand before they start to speak and wait for the facilitator to point to them. Then there are others who might directly challenge what's being said, or simply jump in with their viewpoint.

Solutions

There are several things you can do to overcome these cultural barriers:

1. Create rituals at the start of your meeting. That means setting ground rules for the session and being very clear on how you expect people to behave and engage in the session. That could be saying things like, 'Turn your video camera on and raise your hand if you've got any questions during the session.' Or being broader in setting out your ground rules, such as by telling the participants that you expect them to be open-minded, or you expect them to contribute, or you expect them to just listen in.
2. Evaluate the meeting format. Ask the participants for some input on the process and ask them afterwards how they felt the session went. Make sure you're always learning about

what worked well and what you can improve for next time. Often people worry that they'll receive negative feedback, but frequently we find that what you're feeling as the facilitator will be very different from the perspective of the participants. You need to evaluate and be open about where you are in the learning process. Don't be afraid of admitting that this is a new space for you as well (if it is!).

3. Make sure that you're involving all the participants throughout the meeting.
4. Check in on the decisions that are made, both during the meeting and after it has finished.

Technological distance

In a virtual session, you have more to think about when it comes to technology. In a physical meeting space, you might have difficulty connecting to an external screen or turning the projector on, but that is likely to be about the only technical difficulty that you face. In a virtual setting you have to consider all the problems you could have, including with your wifi connection, VPN issues, your audio or camera not working (or both!), a link not working, issues with access to the collaboration tools or even your computer having a virus. There are many more things, either on your side or that of the participants, that can get in the way of engagement in a session.

Solutions

There are several things you can do to overcome these technological barriers:

1. Do your preparation before a session and make sure that you know your equipment and tools. Know how you'll mute and

unmute participants, know how you'll open the links (and test that they work). Know how you can resolve issues for your participants too, such as a link not working or opening, or sound not working.

2. Do a test run with everything before the session. Do this with someone attending the session if possible so that you can identify any potential issues for your participants, such as a VPN tunnel or something that could cause issues when they're logging in. The larger the sessions that you're running, the more important this becomes.

3. Ask your participants to test their equipment the day before the session and to contact you if they have any questions.

4. Invite people to the meeting five or ten minutes before it's due to start so that you can have an informal talk and test that their webcam, audio and everything else is working. You can also take the first five or ten minutes of the session to teach your participants about the core functionalities of the technology so that they know how to use the platform during the session. This is especially relevant if they are new to the software.

5. Make sure you have a Plan B in case there are serious technical difficulties. That could be as simple as taking a ten-minute break to solve a technical issue and then getting everyone to log back in.

6. Send out all the documentation after the meeting to anyone who couldn't attend.

7. Make sure you're sitting in a quiet place where you won't be disturbed, and ask your participants to do the same.

8. Mute individual participants during the session if there are any disturbances.

Discover your level of organisational maturity in the virtual space

We want you to evaluate your organisational maturity in the digital space as a prerequisite to hosting good virtual sessions. You can analyse your organisation's virtual maturity through three different lenses: system, process and behaviour. Reflect on the following questions to start exploring how advanced your systems, processes and behaviours are:

System – this is about the hardware and software you use when working virtually

- How good are the computer, webcam, microphone and wifi connection? At your place? with the participants?
- Do you have working video conference tools that support your needs?
  (E.g. Teams, Zoom, Meetup, Slack etc.)
- Do you have software for collaboration and is it updated?
- Do you have participant engagement tools?
  (E.g. At our organisation we use Zoom, Menti and Slido.)

Process – this is about how you communicate and facilitate virtual sessions

- Do you have a defined way of collaborating and communicating internally via mail, Slack, Yammer teams etc.? Is it project related?
- Do you have guidelines for running virtual workshops?
- Do you always have an agenda?

- Do you evaluate your sessions afterwards?
- Do you have a toolbox providing a variety of different processes that you can apply to different sorts of virtual meetings?

Behaviour – this is about how people behave in virtual sessions, both the facilitator and the participants

- What does the virtual meeting culture at your organisation look like?
- Do your employees have the skills to use the technical platform?
- How well prepared are you, as the facilitator?
- Do people turn on their videos during online sessions? If not, why not?
- Are participants active during meetings or do they tend to get distracted?
- Do you have high energy or do you just log on and talk through your slides?

Here are two examples of organisations that have different maturity levels in relation to their virtual meeting culture.

The international retail store

This organisation has a slow virtual private network (VPN). As a result, they don't use video in their online meetings because the connection is not good enough. The company has Office 365 but the employees don't know how to use it to work collaboratively. They send documents back and forth rather than co-creating and editing the same document. Communication in most meetings is one-way. There are often 50+ slides in virtual presentations. Finally, there are few interactions during the sessions.

Evaluation

- *System:* The system isn't fit for purpose for virtual meetings because it doesn't allow the participants to use their videos, and the lack of knowledge of the software restricts their ability to collaborate virtually.
- *Process:* There isn't any clear guidance about how to facilitate virtual meetings, and those leading the session aren't adapting their process for the virtual environment. The way they are working with Office 365 is inefficient.
- *Behaviour:* Participants aren't engaged in the virtual meetings because they aren't being asked to contribute. As they don't have their videos on, there is a high likelihood that they are multitasking.
- *Result:* This organisation does not have a high level of virtual maturity. It isn't thinking consciously about the virtual space and how to use it most effectively.

The medium-sized company

This company is using asynchronous communication technology, with a clearly defined communication channel. They have frequent virtual meetings and the agenda for each meeting is sent out beforehand. The facilitator role is agreed on and there are templates for how to host a virtual meeting, including evaluating the meeting afterwards.

Evaluation

- *System:* The system is robust and supports the virtual environment, allowing all participants to use their videos and work collaboratively during sessions.

- *Process:* There is a clear process for running virtual meetings with the template. Roles are clearly defined and both the facilitators and participants are prepared for each session. Every person in the meeting understands what they need to achieve because this is clearly set out in the agenda. They also know how they are going to achieve their goals.
- *Behaviour:* Participants are engaged in the session and encouraged to contribute. By evaluating each meeting, the facilitator ensures that improvements are made to future sessions to keep engagement high.
- *Result:* This organisation has a high level of virtual maturity. It is thinking carefully about how to maximise the virtual space and deliver a better experience for all those involved in each meeting.

Build capabilities for virtual collaboration

It's important for businesses of all sizes to understand that transitioning to the virtual environment is just like any other capability building exercise. Organisations need to select which platforms to use, and develop these competencies not only among facilitators, but also in general among the people who will be attending virtual meetings. They need to ensure that everyone is confident in using these virtual platforms.

In some organisations, not all of the workforce will need to be trained to deliver and attend virtual meetings, because their jobs are very much based in the physical world. But there are other organisations where using the virtual space effectively could benefit the majority, if not all, of their employees. It's important to evaluate to what degree your organisation needs to adopt virtual environments.

One of the challenges for larger organisations is that they tend not to be as agile as small and medium-sized businesses.

Many businesses that were born in the last five years have just adopted the virtual as part of their way of working from the out-set. But larger, longer-established organisations often can't adapt as quickly. They often have many different systems and this adds a layer of complexity to the process. Typically there isn't any guidance about how to use these systems, and people are just thrown into them.

Often these organisations are aware of the cool tools available for virtual working, but there isn't enough focus on change management to encourage people to learn how to use them effectively. This requires a specific focus to be a successful transformation.

Applying virtual meetings to different situations

Moving into the virtual space doesn't only have to apply to inter-nal meetings, workshops and training. For example, businesses could explore virtual sales and how to sell to clients virtually. In a small organisation, where there is no perceived need for going virtual internally, there could be significant opportunities to go virtual in order to reach clients. In this instance, the business might be able to significantly increase the number of potential clients it can reach out to if it operates in the virtual world.

There can also be applications for using the virtual space with vendors, clients, buyers and partners. You don't need to just think of going virtual in the internal context of your organisa-tion, but can look outside as well.

3

The Virtual Facilitator

The virtual facilitator can be anyone in an organisation who is responsible for a meeting or a workshop. As the facilitator, you will be the person running the session. Virtual facilitation is not easy – the facilitator has to run the process, control the tech and always needs to be 'above the process', which means they are constantly considering whether the current activities are bringing the group closer to their shared goal.

From experience, we know that virtual facilitation is a skill to be trained in and learned. You might even call it an essential twenty-first-century skill.

Developing the skills for virtual facilitation

Some people might believe that they either have what it takes or they don't to be a facilitator. We believe that anyone can train themselves to be a good virtual facilitator. There is a lot of work involved in this process and you need to get as much experience as you can. Gaining this experience primarily comes from facilitating sessions. The knowledge we're sharing with you in this book is only part of the process – you need to apply this many times for it to become a skill.

You need certain knowledge, such as how to design your meetings in a brain-friendly and effective way, and you need to know about the tech side of things too, such as the platform you're working with and how best to use it. You also need to know about your participants, and this will, of course, change between each session.

But the more experience you have as a facilitator, the more you will develop these skills and your understanding. You need to put in the hours, ask for feedback and be honest about where you still need to improve and develop. Being a virtual facilitator isn't just something you can 'do' – it's important to train, learn and gain experience in this field if you want to host good meetings and sessions. From our perspective organisations working increasingly virtually should seriously address this as part of their internal capability building program.

Key traits of good virtual facilitators

One of the most important traits of a good virtual facilitator is having emotional intelligence, and knowing how to apply this empathetic social intelligence in a virtual space where you don't have a physical connection to the other people in the session.

It's important to have an insight into the psychology of human processes. From experience we know that people won't learn or adopt new behaviours if they are just being told what to do. As a virtual facilitator, it's not about you giving a great PowerPoint presentation and explaining your slides clearly. It's about how your presentation is perceived and what the participants in the session do as a result.

As a virtual facilitator self-awareness and situational awareness are other skills to grow. In terms of self-awareness, that means you have some perception of what you bring into the (virtual) room and know how you impact others. This could be knowing your own values, behaviours and intents and how those could potentially influence a session.

In terms of situational awareness, you need to be able to analyse the situation and always be aware of what's happening around you. This is important to make sure you move towards the purpose together with your participants. If there is something disturbing the progress, it's your job to handle it. Therefore being curious, both in terms of yourself and the situation, is a key aspect of being a good facilitator.

> *Top tip: Being a good virtual facilitator is about being interested instead of being interesting.*

Knowledge of the tech is secondary to your 'soft skills'

Of course you need to know and understand your tech to a certain level, but this isn't the most important aspect for being a good virtual facilitator. In fact, you can even divide the technology role from the facilitation role if you have two people running the meeting. One can be a pure facilitator, while the other can run the tech. If you have the luxury (or a very large session), you could even introduce a third person as a co-facilitator.

How to separate the roles and responsibilities

As soon as you have more than ten people in a session, we recommend considering separating the facilitator role so that you have more than one facilitator (Figure 3.1).

Lead facilitator	Co-Facilitator	Technical assistant
• Design the workshop • Prepare slides • Present • Facilitate discussions • Set context for exercises • Debrief exercises	• Co-train content • Facilitate exercises • Monitor and answer chat • Give feedback on the process	• Set up the room for the facilitators • Help participants with technical issues • Set up micro-involvements & exercises

Figure 3.1   Separating roles and responsibilities

The role of the lead facilitator

This person will have responsibility for how the session is run and will take the decisions about how to move it forward. The lead facilitator will be the one who primarily features on screen. They will start discussions and also close them down. They'll set the context for exercises. They'll be the one who manages the back and forth between all the participants in the session. They'll also be responsible for making sure that the session stays on track – in terms of time – by moving people forward. They will be responsible for debriefing afterwards. It's important to only have one lead facilitator.

The role of the co-facilitator

This person is there to support the lead facilitator and to give them the option of stepping out should they need to. The co-facilitator may co-facilitate one part of the agenda. Or they can be the person who leads an exercise. For example, the lead facilitator can tee up the exercise and explain the context, but the co-facilitator can then step in and help people to move forwards and generally facilitate these exercises. The co-facilitator can also be responsible for monitoring the chat. They can check if there are any questions that need to be answered and bring these to the attention of the lead facilitator at an appropriate time. You can't speak and write at the same time, so if you will be using the chat function it's a privilege to have a co-facilitator who can help manage it. The co-facilitator can also give feedback on the process and can help to make sure you don't lose track of time. As the lead facilitator, it can be very helpful to have a person supporting you during the session – especially if you are new to virtual facilitation.

The role of the technical assistant

If you have a large session, we strongly recommend having a technical assistant. He or she will help participants deal with any technical issues. They will also be responsible for physically setting up the virtual room and checking the technical side of the session, such as making sure the picture from the webcam and the audio is high quality. They may also set up some of the micro-involvements, such as chats, polls and breakout exercises. Their role will be to make sure that all of this functionality works as it should.

The description of the three roles probably illustrates why, as just one person, you might sometimes struggle in virtual sessions. Our recommendation, if you have the opportunity, is to share the responsibilities to free you up to be present. How you split these roles and responsibilities will depend on the size of your virtual session, as well as your experience as a facilitator.

If you don't have the luxury of having a dedicated co-facilitator or technical assistant, you may want to engage one or more participants to help during the session. You can even build this into the design of your session. You can ask for someone to volunteer for this role at the start of the session. Don't be afraid of engaging them, because people like to own part of the agenda. Whether you need someone to monitor the chat or help with an issue, there will usually be someone who is prepared to step in.

For larger events, we would always recommend that you have a technical assistant and maybe also a co-facilitator to make sure that it is run professionally. If you don't have anyone within your organisation who can fulfill those roles, you may want to hire someone for that purpose to enable you to fully focus on the content as the lead facilitator on the day.

Roles and responsibilities within virtual facilitation

- Lead facilitator: Responsible for the session, sets the scene, runs the process, follows up discussions and holds people responsible for the ground rules.
- Co-facilitator: Runs part of the agenda, gives feedback on the progress to the lead facilitator, monitors the chat and other communication channels.
- Technical assistant: Controls the tech, sets up the physical room and helps the participants with technical issues.

Knowing your 'dances' in virtual facilitation

Imagine that you're practicing ballroom dancing. Firstly, you need to know which dances you are going to be dancing and then you need to know who your partner will be for each dance.

Of course you need to master the different dances, but if you're not aware of which dance you're attempting from the beginning then it's going to be a mess. Being aware of your role within a session is crucial, especially if that role is as the facilitator (Figure 3.2). Telling your participants about it can be just as important.

We want you to think of the different roles you need to master within a meeting as different types of dances. One of those 'dances' will be that of the **facilitator,** where you need to get the participants talking and doing things. Another 'dance' would be as an **advisor or expert.** That's a totally different type of dance, where you need a different set of capabilities to those of the facilitator.

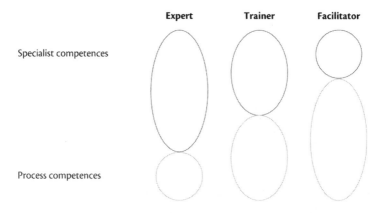

Figure 3.2   Knowing your dances as facilitator

- The first dance is pure **facilitation** is where you're only in control of the process and you need the participants in the session to provide the content or expertise. In this case you're not.providing the content, but instead guiding the process. It can be very valuable to have an outsider with no power relation in the organisation and 'no opinion' on the subject to run the process and ensure progress. Both because it can make it easier to guide the process and as it's a huge task in itself to control all of the elements that we'll discuss later in the book, such as energy, the direction of the meeting or how to cope with resistance in the space.

- Being an **expert** is a totally different dance. This means that you are a specialist and provide content for the session. Quite often this also includes having an opinion on decisions or effect of the meeting. If the formal facilitator is also the expert during a meeting it can be hard to guide the process in an objective way, engage participants and also to stay on top of the content and the process.
- Another 'dance' you might need to master is that of being a **trainer or teacher**, where there's a goal or where you need the participants to learn something new. This is different to being a facilitator, because there is a right or wrong outcome in that situation which has been defined.

As well as being aware of the different 'dances' you might need to perform, you also need to be aware of which of those 'dances' you are required to perform at this particular moment. Are you expected to come into the session as an advisor or expert who has a solution or an argument; or are you expected to facilitate the process? If your 'dance' doesn't align with what is expected of you, it will be a poor meeting.

One challenge we see people encounter when they are facilitating a session is that they aren't aware of their own self-interest in the solution. Because they are very interested in the solution, or have maybe already made a decision about the direction they'll take as a manager or business leader, it is difficult for them to be a pure facilitator.

If you are really good at 'dancing', you can blend the different 'dances' together. The ultimate aim is that you could perform different 'dances' in the same meeting, but if you do that you need to clearly communicate when you are shifting from one 'dance' to the next.

Within the context of a virtual meeting where you are the facilitator, it might mean that you step out of that role to become an expert and speak on a topic for ten minutes, and then step back into your role as the facilitator. The key to doing this effectively is to ensure that not only are you aware when you switch roles, but that everyone else in the session is too.

When you forget to tell everyone else which 'dance' you're performing, or which role you're in at different points in the session, it leads to confusion. This in turn may mean that participants resist the new 'dance' you've introduced, and that can make it more difficult to achieve the end result that you're looking for.

Case

The problem

We were working as part of a group of 30 people to co-create a new HR system. The project owner was among the group, but he was also the team facilitator. After the session, he was complaining that there wasn't much input from the rest of the team. He didn't feel as though they were contributing. They were struggling to reach any decisions and he felt like he had to drag everything out of them.

What he did not realise was that this was turning into a power game. The project owner wasn't on the same level as the other participants and that was making it difficult for him to facilitate the session.

The solution

We introduced an external facilitator. The external facilitator stopped people talking too much, actively encouraged others to share their thoughts and participate, and opened the conversation up. The facilitator was also able to draw the discussion back to the point in hand and prevent people from deviating too much from the purpose. This allowed everyone to contribute more equally and provided space for those who were reluctant to open up. It was also valuable for the project owner, who now had some free conscious space to be fully present as he wasn't focusing on facilitating the session.

Master the entire 'dancefloor'

The other element of knowing the 'dances' of virtual facilitation is understanding the wider context. To be a good facilitator, you need to master the entire 'dancefloor'. This is about where you are putting your focus. Your focus could be on the business, on the people, on the process, on the long term, or in the moment and what's happening today. Each of these areas of focus is like a section of the 'dancefloor' and as the facilitator you need to know what's happening in every part of your 'dancefloor'.

Some people have a preference for being much more in the moment with people, while others prefer to approach things from a strategic business perspective. A really good facilitator will bridge these dimensions and have a broad overview of how what they're doing today links to the future. They'll understand that if they want certain changes to happen with the behaviour of the people, this will also have X, Y, Z effect on the business.

Elements of the virtual facilitator's toolbox

Below are the key elements that should be in every virtual facilitator's toolbox. We'll unpack each of these in more detail in Part II, Part III and Part IV.

- Virtual process methods.
- Understanding of the virtual space and tech requirements.
- Questioning techniques and response formats virtually:
  - Answer yourself
  - Ask the audience
  - Poll the audience
  - Always follow-up: did that answer your question?
- Create energy during the session.
- Micro-involvements.
- Virtual communication.
- Feedback methods in the virtual space, and ensuring you don't miss feedback from participants.
- Presenting techniques in the virtual space, including PowerPoint and body language.
- Decision-making in the virtual space.
- Understanding of preferences and learning styles.

Self-assessment: How skilled are you as a virtual facilitator?

Now that you better understand the role of the virtual facilitator, it is a good time to reflect on your own skill levels to help you understand where and how you can improve. Reflect on the following questions honestly, to highlight what you are already good at and where you can improve.

System

1. Do you have one shared platform?

2. How good would you say you are at working in it?

3. Have you got a webcam and a facility to host and participate in virtual meetings?

4. Do you have software to create polls, breakout rooms, interactive documents and chat?

5. How would you rate yourself at using these tools?

6. Do you ensure your participants are ready to join the platform used for the session?

7. Do you help your participants during your sessions when tech issues occur?

Process

1. Have you been trained in virtual facilitation?

2. Do you have a 'toolbox' with different virtual process methods to design your meeting or workshop?

3. Do you use an agenda during meetings?

4. Do you revisit it for each step?

5. How often do you set ground rules in your virtual meetings?

6. Do you set corner flags for your sessions?

7. Do you explain the context of your sessions?

8. Do you ensure trust and connection between your participants?

9. Do you provide clarity over your own role during your sessions?

10. Do you ensure you have breaks every 45 minutes?

Behaviour

1. Are you aware of your physical presence during your sessions? Do you design for this considering the likes of your background, clothing and light?

2. Do you check if people are actively participating in your virtual sessions (e.g. via chat, thumbs up, energy check-ins or group work with 'things to produce')?

3. Do you have a way of organising oral and text inputs from participants during your session?

4

The Tech Setup (General)

You can easily drown in the search for the perfect technical solution, leaving no time to plan and prepare your session or even learn the new platform. We believe virtual facilitation is about humanising the virtual space, not about the technology itself. Our suggestion is to select one that you know works and learn how to get the best out of it. In addition, you can use smaller user-friendly interaction tools if they are not already part of your platform (such as menti.com).

Removing the entry barrier

The reason why we recommend using technology that you already have and know is twofold. The first reason is that you need to master the technology yourself. It is simply easier to learn if you stick to one core platform. The second reason is that this removes what we call the entry barrier for your participants. The entry barrier means that new tools take energy to learn. When you want to introduce your employees to something new, you'll often see many of them shying away and saying, 'I don't know it, I don't like it.' Minimising the entry barrier is key to making sure you don't lose people at this early stage.

This is why we strongly recommend using tech that you already have in place. Often there will be more possibilities within your existing platform than you know. If you are missing some features in the platform, technology or hardware that you have, more often than not you can find a workaround or a simple and user-friendly add-on that will deliver the functionality you need.

Top tips for introducing new technology

If you need to introduce a new platform, be aware that there will be some change management around this decision. You will need to invest time for both you and the participants to learn and master this new platform. You also need to consider the financial investment required to acquire the platform you want to use. Always remember that it will take time for you to become efficient with a new platform and to be comfortable with the possibilities it presents.

If you choose to introduce a new platform for your session, we recommend doing the following:

- Set up a prep session a day or a week before you expect your participants to use it for the first time. Consider whether this should be voluntary or mandatory, based on the perceived skills of your participants (and the variation between them).
- Give them a tour of the platform and allow them to play around with it.
- Share a video introduction or similar if it exists.
- Do a short tour, demonstrating the platform in the beginning of your session, making sure participants try the features in practice.

The advantage for the participants is that when they join the first virtual session, they aren't experiencing the software and technology for the first time. This will make them feel more comfortable both before and during the session. We strongly believe in doing all that you can as an organisation to remove these entry barriers.

The advantage for you as the facilitator is that it gives you an opportunity to identify issues you and your participants are likely to experience. Without running a practice session like this, it can be hard to find out what specific issues people are likely to have beforehand. If you are familiar with the platform, you probably know many of the common issues already. Yet you can't always perceive what the issues will be, because to you the solutions might be obvious. There are also many things you can't foresee. Testing your new platform with your participants from the specific organisation is a key element of the preparation phase for virtual sessions.

The key thing to remember is that whenever you're introducing a new tech setup, you need to be careful about how you do it.

Which platform(s) (software) to use?

When it comes to virtual facilitation and meeting other people in a virtual space, there are several tools that you may want to invest in. Most importantly, you need to have a video conferencing tool where you are able to talk and see participants in real time. You may also want to have a tool that allows virtual collaboration, such as a virtual whiteboard, shared document, shared PowerPoint file or a polling tool. Finally, you may also want to consider having a place where you can communicate in an asynchronised way. In addition to the key tools, we use a range of smaller, user-friendly tools for polling, word clouds, quizzes etc. The use of these depends very much on your selection of your key platform(s), as well as your skills as a virtual facilitator.

You may not always need all of these tools. Sometimes you'll want to have the video and a collaboration tool. Other times you'll just want to have video, and other times you'll just want a virtual whiteboard. The key is having them available when you need to use them.

How to choose a video conference platform

There are many great video conferencing tools available. When you are looking for a platform, ask yourself the following questions:

1. What do I/my organisation already have/use?
2. How easy is it to use for the participants and the facilitator (both with regards to signing up and using during the session)?
3. How smooth is the onboarding process?
4. How does it integrate with my existing software technology? (E.g. MS Teams, Google Suite, Android, Apple.)
5. How well does the tool support my process needs?
6. How easy is it to interact with all the participants? Does it offer chat, polls, non-verbal feedback and/or breakout sessions?
7. How reliable is it in my geographical location?
8. How much does it cost for the facilitator? And is there any cost for participants?

Our top video conferencing tools

- Zoom
- Hangout
- Teams
- Adobe Connect
- Google Meet

We have made a short comparison of the video conferencing tools we prefer that you can find online. www.implement. dk/vf#tech

Why use a virtual whiteboard platform?

Research shows that handwriting and drawing increases a person's ability to think creatively, solve problems and retain knowledge. The activities of writing and drawing engage the brain in ways that typing and texting don't, so you may find that inviting your team to join in with a whiteboard session on your next video conference could be just the breakthrough you need to tap into their more innovative ideas – or to do sketches at their own desk and show them on the camera. We believe that this visualisation of virtual meetings is incredibly valuable. We'd argue that combining the physical and virtual designs or introducing the virtual whiteboards should be used in many more of our meetings, instead of only talking.

When you are talking together in a virtual session it can be challenging to have a discussion, not to repeat too much, and for all the participants to understand clearly what you are talking about and what the outcomes of that discussion are. One of the benefits of virtual whiteboards is that you can easily create a visual output of your discussions.

These tools replace the likes of physical whiteboards, Post-it notes, or even just people writing their thoughts on their own pieces of paper and comparing them later. Virtual whiteboards are also an excellent tool to replace a full journey or project stand-up wall. The advantage of a virtual whiteboard in this situation is that it allows you to see the full overview, but then also enables you to zoom into specific elements of the project and show smaller details.

Our top virtual whiteboard tools

- Google Jamboard
- Padlet
- Miro
- PowerPoint

We have made a short comparison of the whiteboard tools we prefer that you can find online. www.implement.dk/vf#tech

How to evaluate virtual whiteboard providers

There are a few questions you should ask when deciding which virtual whiteboard will be best suited to your session:

1. What do I already use/ What does my organisation already have/ What do participants use?

2. How interactive do you want the board to be? Is it mostly you as the facilitator who wants to visualise the journey or make the to-do list? Or does this need to be a space where everyone can co-create a lot of content?

3. How many sessions will it be used for? Is it a one-time thing, or do you want people to use it multiple times? If you want people to use it multiple times, is it worth investing in the pro features? For a single session, will making people sign up for a platform prevent them from using it?

4. How much content do you expect to create? How much detail will you want to include on it? Will there be a lot of ideas or just a few points?

Why use virtual polling tools?

Event interaction and networking apps are becoming increasingly popular. As a facilitator, this gives you an excellent opportunity to hear from all the participants very quickly. These tools provide a great way for you to get more interaction in your sessions and for everyone to be heard and seen in your meetings.

Polling tools allow everyone to interact instantly on any matter you decide. When we use these tools, we notice that people feel like they are owning part of the meeting, that they are influencing it and they can influence it very quickly. These tools also provide an opportunity to introduce an element of gamification to sessions, especially where you are short on time, for instance by limiting the amount of time participants have to give their answers.

Polling tools can also be a useful way of introducing psychological safety to your virtual sessions, by allowing participants to remain anonymous. They don't need to raise their hand to make their voice heard, but these tools give them a way to put their words out there without being identified. In our experience, there is a much higher chance that everyone will be involved when we use anonymous polling tools, because the participants aren't worried about standing out from the crowd and are allowed to see what other people think of a question or issue.

In a physical meeting there are cues that you can see in other participants to know that you're not alone. Someone else might be nodding at what's being said, for example. But in this setting it's much harder to know what everyone in the room or the audience is thinking. These polling tools allow everyone to see how the whole audience is feeling about an issue.

What's more, tech-savvy attendees expect to use mobile event apps at events and conferences to do everything from check the agenda to using various interaction tools like Q&A, tasks or networking features. Conference apps allow you to deliver a personalised experience at scale. But some of the most interesting outcomes from professional conferences are the insights gained from fellow attendees. Polling is one of the key ways to check the pulse of an event's audience. Thanks to advances in technology, what was once a subjective count of raised hands has transformed into highly accurate surveys delivering real-time data.

Our top virtual polling tools

- Poll Anywhere
- Sli.dO
- Mentimeter.com
- Kahoot

We have made a short comparison of the polling tools we prefer that you can find online. www.implement.dk/vf#tech

How to evaluate polling tools

Choosing the right polling tools for your session will depend on your needs within a specific session. Some of the options available are better for big events. Some are designed for quizzing. Others are designed for large groups. Here are a few questions to ask yourself when choosing a polling tool (or tools) for your session:

1. What do I/my organisation already have/use?
2. Are you looking for a platform that will provide Q&A functionality?
3. Do you want a platform that will allow participants to provide open answers?
4. Will you be conducting a quiz or is it just for a simple poll?
5. How can participants access the content before, during and after the session?
6. What other functionalities might you need? E.g. breakout rooms, micro-interactions.

Advice for using virtual polling tools

Using virtual polling tools introduces another potential layer of complexity for you as the virtual facilitator. If you're using polling tools such as those we've described, you may want to consider having a co-facilitator or technical assistant to help manage this and ensure that you don't become less efficient as a facilitator because of the introduction of additional tools.

It's also important to understand how valuable this data can be to you when you're the facilitator, because it gives you a much clearer view of where your participants are in terms of their engagement and energy, which is something we'll cover later in the book. What using virtual polling tools does is help you to see how people are feeling about a question. They also help you to spark conversations and they give you concrete information that you can use to decide how best to proceed with the session.

Using a Q&A function, for instance, can allow people to ask questions that they may not feel comfortable asking if you were all together in person, which can be a good way to speak about and tackle challenging issues. However, the anonymity these tools offer can be a downside, because people will typically take greater ownership of a question if it's one they ask out loud, rather than via a digital tool. As the facilitator, you need to be aware that negative energy and resistance can creep into sessions if these tools aren't used wisely. Particularly it's important how you frame and formulate the questions within your virtual polling tools, as your questions affects the answers. The specific wording you use for the question can have a tremendous impact on the outcome you get and the feeling/mindset that you leave participants with afterwards.

Suggested setups for a facilitator's hardware

When it comes to the hardware side of facilitating, having the right equipment makes a huge difference. The good news is you can create these setups with just a little investment, and this will have a big impact on the quality of your sessions. You can scale it up from a very small setup to a very large setup. We have provided examples of a small, medium and large setup to give you an indication of what is required for different types of sessions. For participants, we would recommend that you advise them to use the small setup.

What all of these setups have in common is that they include the elements of audio, a microphone, a camera, lighting and a display. There is a huge variety of hardware and products that you can buy, so we aren't going to recommend any specific items.

What we would recommend is that you look at what's new and search from there.

The small setup

This is the setup that most participants will use in their everyday meetings (Figure 4.1).

One thing to note is the use of an external headset. We strongly recommend using an external headset for your audio. Although the microphone that's built into the computer is okay, it isn't more than that. If you're going to facilitate, and many people will have to listen to you, we strongly recommend putting on a headset with an external microphone to ensure proper sound quality. Having the microphone close to your mouth also makes a huge difference in terms of minimising background noise. Finally, it tends to remove some of the echoes you can have on a call.

In terms of lighting, you should try to have natural light whenever possible. Many people make the mistake of placing themselves in an office with the light coming from behind them or from the side. This means it is either too dark to properly see your facial expression or you appear to have two faces, where one side of your face is really visible, but you cannot see the other part. We recommend having natural light coming from in front of you. Facing a window to allow the light in from that angle will usually do it.

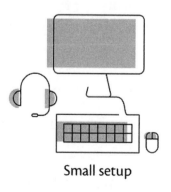

Small setup

Figure 4.1 The small setup

We also recommend raising up your computer so that you don't have the angle of looking down on people. Most people tend to open their laptop and tilt it up. This means that other people are almost looking up your nose. That's a bad perspective to have because it can appear that you're talking down to them. We recommend putting your laptop on a box and having an external mouse and keyboard.

Water, coffee and snacks can support your physical energy. Make sure they are within easy reach of your computer but not in positions where they will get in the way or could be knocked over easily.

Use the link for a virtual tour of the setup: www.implement. dk/vf#tech

The medium setup

As soon as you get closer to sessions of around ten people, or when you move into virtual workshops or virtual training, you may want to consider going for a medium setup (Figure 4.2). This will allow you to easily balance more interactions.

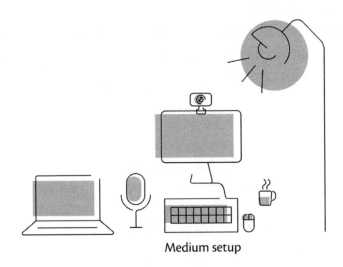

Medium setup

Figure 4.2   The medium setup

As with the small setup, you should have either an external headset or an external microphone that's positioned on the table. We recommend having a separate webcam in this setup. That's because the webcams that are built into laptops aren't particularly high quality. If you have an external webcam you can choose one that is full HD. This makes a difference in terms of people being able to see everything in your facial expressions. Also in this setup we recommend you add some extra light, to ensure the colour of your face is warm and your facial expressions are visible.

We also recommend having a stand-up desk for this setup. This allows you to move freely with your body and means that everyone can see your full body and not just your face from the neck up. When you're using this setup, we'd suggest standing a little bit back from the desk to enable the webcam to capture more of your body.

In terms of the display, we'd recommend having two screens. This allows you to have a screen that you can present on, while using the second screen to display your notes, view timers and your chat, and from where you can drag in polls at relevant points in the meeting.

If you are hosting many virtual sessions in your organisation, you may want to consider creating something like this as a stationary studio in a meeting room to save setting it up each time.

Use the link for a virtual tour of the setup: www.implement. dk/vf#tech

The large setup

You'll want to use the large setup when you're facilitating large-scale meetings, which usually means for groups of 50 people or more (Figure 4.3).

In this setup you're going to want a high-quality microphone that stands on the desk – to have more freedom to move,

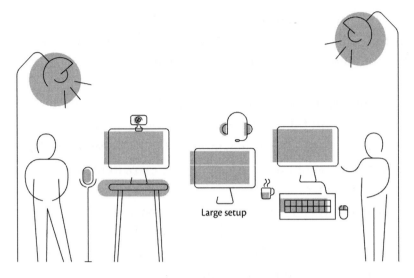

Figure 4.3   The large setup

higher-quality sound, and to avoid using the headset, which can look a little unprofessional. You can still do fine with a webcam, but you may also want to consider using a DSLR camera. If you want to move around while you're facilitating, you may need a cameraperson and it's best to mount the camera on a tripod to keep the picture steady. This is really important if you want to have multiple whiteboards that you use, or if you want to move around in your office or between your displays. Using a DSLR also provides a cinematic look and greater depth of field, allowing your face to be in greater focus and for the background to be blurred.

In terms of the lighting in this setup, you want to have two lights set up to shine from each side in order to remove shadows. You could use softboxes or ring lights.

You will also want to have three display screens. One of these is for monitoring the next slide, whilst the second is where you can see all of the participants on the same screen. The third screen is for your notes, chat, videos to play during the session etc.

For this level of setup, you will want to have a technical assistant who can be presenting that additional screen for you, getting the next slide ready and taking care of the technical side of the session.

This setup, and the other two, can be adjusted to meet your needs and to suit different situations.

Use the link for a virtual tour of the setup: www.implement. dk/vf#tech

Think about your background

Take the time to check your background. You don't need to have a clinical white background; in fact it's nice to add human touches like a plant or a poster, especially if it relates to what you're talking about. The main thing you want to achieve with your background is to provide some atmosphere without being distracting. It shouldn't pull people's attention away from you. Try to make it professional and tidy. If you're working from home, you can always blur your background if you would prefer, but we think it's fine to show that you're in an office environment.

For larger setups, you might want to design the background intentionally with plants, furniture etc. or explore the advances with green screens that allow you to share PowerPoints that you can interact with, or to show movies.

Your setup as a participant

As we've already said, the small setup is sufficient as a participant, but there are a couple of other things to consider. The most important thing is to make sure that you're in a setting where there will be no disturbances, such as a quiet area. You should

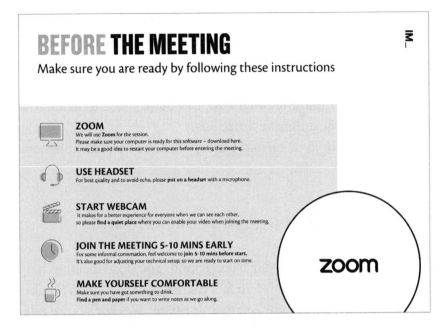

BEFORE THE MEETING
Make sure you are ready by following these instructions

ZOOM
We will use **Zoom** for the session.
Please make sure your computer is ready for this software – download here.
It may be a good idea to restart your computer before entering the meeting.

USE HEADSET
For best quality and to avoid echo, please **put on a headset** with a microphone.

START WEBCAM
It makes for a better experience for everyone when we can see each other,
so please **find a quiet place** where you can enable your video when joining the meeting.

JOIN THE MEETING 5-10 MINS EARLY
For some informal conversation, feel welcome to **join 5-10 mins before start.**
It's also good for adjusting your technical setup, so we are ready to start on time.

MAKE YOURSELF COMFORTABLE
Make sure you have got something to drink.
Find a pen and paper if you want to write notes as we go along.

zoom

Figure 4.4   Help your participants get ready

have light coming from in front of you so that people can see your face. Make sure you enable your webcam, because that's a big part of engaging. We want you to help improve the quality of the session, so make sure you have a headset or a good quality microphone close to you.

Another rule is that it should be one person per device. Having several people crowded around the same computer doesn't create the right conditions for a good meeting where participants are fully involved, e.g. in the chat. Remember to inform participants prior to the session. We do it in the invitation as illustrated in Figure 4.4.

Setting participants' expectations

If you plan certain activities that will require participants to use a computer and not a smartphone, make sure you set these expectations clearly before the meeting. If you don't, then you may find participants join you from mobile phones while they're on the move. That might mean they aren't able to contribute to collaborative documents, for instance. It's important as the facilitator that you align everyone's expectations about how to participate in your session.

5

Wrapping Up the Before Part

Now that you've finished reading about the essentials, you'll hopefully have an idea of what facilitation is all about and have an idea what a virtual facilitator looks like. We'll go much more into the role of the facilitator during the rest of the book. Also we hope that you learned about the virtual space, what it looks like, what it offers and how you can take advantage of this. Finally we provided you with the basic insights on the tech side of things. This is basic stuff that you need to master, but just to make it clear once and again – virtual facilitation is more than technology. It's about humans.

To help you get an overview we have collected our top takeaways from each chapter. These are things we think are especially important.

Chapter	Top takeaways
1: An Introduction to Virtual Facilitation	• Use the Five Levels of Involvement to think about what type of session you should go for and how you should involve your participants. This could be a meeting, a workshop, a training session or a large-scale get-together. • Be clear about the corner flags of your session as well as the playing field to be focused in that particular session; be clear in your communication and avoid pseudo-involvement. • Put your session into the wider context of your project and/or within the organisation to help see the bigger purpose.
2: Going Virtual with Your Session	• The essentials around facilitation also apply in a virtual setting. • Get acquainted with the opportunities and limitations of virtual sessions to make the best use of the format. • Look at your (virtual) meeting culture: What does it look like? • Build your own capabilities for virtual facilitation – it's a twenty-first-century skill.
3: The Virtual Facilitator	• Be aware of the role you play during the session. Are you the facilitator, expert or trainer? Do you need to switch roles during the session? • Your tech skills are part of your toolbox, but your facilitation skills comes first. • Is one facilitator enough for your session or do you need a co-facilitator, a technical assistant or both? • Do a self-assessment: How skilled are you within virtual facilitation?

Chapter	Top takeaways
4: The Tech Setup	• Remove or minimise the entry barrier for your participants.
	• Use a platform that you and your participants already know if possible.
	• Make sure you have the right hardware such as screen, headset, webcam and a decent location to broadcast from.
	• Help your participants to arrange themselves and their hardware.

11

Before – Designing for Effect

For any good session, be it small or large, short or long, a few participants or many, you need to go through three phases: before the session, during the session and after the session.

Now we're going to dig into the before phase, which is all about planning a good session. If there's one essential idea to take from this section, it's that so much of the impact and quality of a good session lies in the before phase. This takes time, and we strongly encourage you to prioritise this. Not only if you're new to virtual facilitation, but also as you become more experienced. That's because the more experienced you become, the more tempted you are to think that you can manage your way through a session without doing much planning. But without the right preparation, you won't have a high-quality session.

In this part of the book, we'll introduce you to useful tools you can use for planning your session, based on the Design Star. The Design Star is a structured approach to designing your session. One of the most crucial aspects of planning any session, especially virtual, is thinking about its purpose. You always need to ask: Why are we here? What impact are we looking for? What is the outcome? Who do we need to involve to get there? How do we need to run it and who needs to play a key role in this? Which platform will support us to get there? (Or platforms, because you might need more than one.) What partners are important to reach the purpose?

The whole idea of the before phase is that the more prepared you are – in terms of understanding why you're running the session, what you want to discuss and how you'll do it and what you want to get out of it – the more likely you are to reach your purpose.

You might wonder how much time you need for the 'before' phase. The first rule of thumb is that you need to spend more time planning than you think. The second rule, in terms of virtual sessions, is that you need to spend at least half the length of the meeting time in the before phase (in reality it often means that you need to spend as much in planning as on the meeting itself).

Having a plan and a structure allows you to have greater capacity and freedom during the session, because you aren't spending any of your energy in the session making a plan while also trying to give your full attention to the process and the people in the session. Therefore you need to have a firm plan before you start. That's not to say you shouldn't abolish or alter the plan, but it's easier to abolish or alter the plan if you have a plan in the first place.

The point is that good sessions are thought through, whether virtual or physical, and they take time to design and plan. When entering the virtual space this is even more important, as we are less flexible during the session or workshop. As such, we believe that investing time and energy in the right design and preparation provides a group with a fast track to results. A clever and well-thought-through process will reduce the number of sessions required and enhance the quality of the ones you do attend.

6

Designing Virtual Meetings and Workshops with Engagement and Effect

As we said in the introduction to this part of the book, any good session needs to be well thought through and well planned, whether it's physical or virtual. In a virtual space, you have less flexibility during a session, which means it's even more important to have a plan. We believe that you need to invest time and energy in designing and preparing every session to make sure that it will achieve the desired outcomes, that everyone will be highly engaged, and that you will have had a big impact.

Many of us have attended too many sessions where we don't feel as though we can make a difference or contribute. This is what we want to change. We want to share our approach to designing sessions with impact. In an overall perspective the preparation process looks like this:

Our approach to designing sessions with impact

1. Go through the Design Star potentially with key stake-holders. It could be your project team, client or other important sponsors. Be especially aware that the purpose matches time, resources and desired effect.

2. Create an agenda for your session, to settle on the overall process.

3. Work through the playbook – a template describing the session with regards to time slots, use of platform and materials, and how each point on the agenda will be handled and by whom.

4. Design your materials, such as PowerPoint, platform(s) and microinteractions and communication to participants (e.g. invitation, preparation tasks and follow-up process)

Check in with your project, client or sponsors as much as needed during the process to qualify it and make sure you are aligned.

During this part we will go through the steps in this process.

The Design Star

The Design Star is a model or structure that helps you devise a high-impact session (Figure 6.1). It helps you to zoom out from the session to create the overall design before you go into the details. The reason we built this model was that we often found that people who were running sessions would just start with the agenda.

This led to sessions that didn't have as much impact or achieve the results they might have done if the time had been taken to just zoom out and ask what the purpose of the session was. However, the Design Star model is about more than just defining the purpose. Once you have that purpose, it's about looking at the various levels and elements you need to support that purpose. Who needs to be involved? Where do we need to have the session? Which platform would support that purpose? Who needs to be brought in, in terms of expertise or decision-making power, and so forth. It's about having that overview of the session. This is very different from starting with a structure like, 'From 9:00–9:30 the manager comes in and gives his state of the union and then we have a Q&A.' Those kinds of sessions are easy to do and easy to run through, but if you really want to make an impact you need to take the time to zoom out and run through this simple model.

The five Ps of the Design Star

There are five elements of the Design Star, which we call the five Ps:

- Purpose
- Participants
- Platform
- Process
- Partners

Use the link to find the template for the Design Star as well as examples of the completed form: www.implement.dk/vf#design

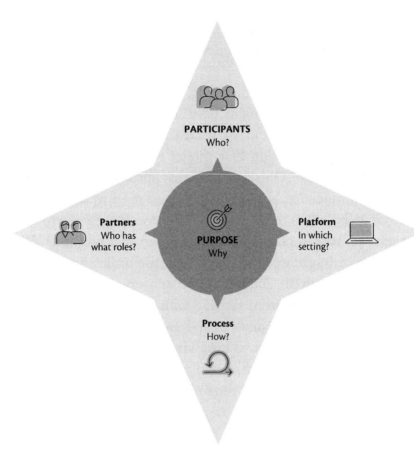

Figure 6.1   The Design Star

Purpose

Purpose is in the middle of the Design Star and it is the most important part. If we were to only give you one takeaway from this entire book, it would be to spend more time on the purpose and asking questions like: Why are we having the session? What does it take for it to be a success? What effect are we looking for? What are the deliverables? It's important to be specific. But you also have to be realistic about what you can achieve in the time you have. We'll talk in greater detail about defining your purpose in the next chapter.

Participants

Once you know the purpose of the session, the next question is: Who needs to join the session to ensure that we achieve that purpose? It might be the entire department, it might be the leaders, the subject matter experts, the users or the clients. The important thing is that there needs to be a link between the purpose and the participants that you can clearly define.

Platform

The next point of the Design Star is platform. In a physical workshop, this would be the environment you're hosting in, such as the meeting room, as well as the mental environment that you want people to join. In the virtual space, you need to decide what platform you want people to join on. This means not only the digital platform where you are hosting the session, but also any other platforms you'll need to use to enable everyone to interact virtually.

The mental platform refers to the mental mindset you want people to have when they're joining your session. Is it a working meeting? Is it a workshop? Is it a reflective setting or is it the event of the year? You want your participants to be mentally prepared in that sense.

Things like this can ensure they not only have the right virtual platform but also the right mental platform for your session, and that they arrive with the right kind of energy. We'll explore this in greater detail in Chapter 9.

Process

Once you know the participants and the platform you'll be using, you need to think about the processes you'll use to run the session. Consider what forms of interactions will be best suited to the people involved and to serving your purpose. You need to think about the process at a high level. It's about knowing that the session will be mostly about information sharing, or that you need to plan for high-level interactions, or that you need to generate data and use polls. We'll explore the process in greater detail in Chapter 10.

Partners

The final point on the Design Star is partners. This has to do with the roles within the session. In some sessions, there might be people who have a special part to play, which means they're not just participants. There will be a facilitator but maybe also a leader, a subject matter expert, somebody taking notes, or a producer. This final element of the Design Star is about aligning those roles, knowing who will play the part of X, Y and Z and engaging them with their part in the session. We take a closer look at this in Chapter 11.

How long does planning take?

The length of time you'll need to spend planning and designing your session will depend on the type of session you're planning for. If it's just a small session, this process takes five or ten minutes to go through the Design Star and a minor effort in the actual planning of the playbook and materials. If it's a large meeting or workshop, you'll spend considerably longer on filling out the Design Star before getting into the extensive and detailed planning.

The five Ps are interdependent

Although the purpose is at the centre of the Design Star, it's important to remember that the purpose, participants, platform, process and partners are all interdependent. Sometimes one point on this Star might be 'fixed', for example you can't use a particular tool due to security, or you can't change the number of participants. In this instance, you need to go back and forth between the different points of the Star and decide what you *can* do, through your session design, to ensure you still get the right outcome. The aim is to make sure that every point on the Design Star is working together to create a really good, productive session.

The Design Star gives you the first design idea for your session. Once you have this, you can decide what your session will look like in terms of the agenda and maybe a playbook but there is still a way to go until your session is planned and designed.

Aim for effect

The Design Star and this process is about going deeper than just the surface of the session. We often encounter people who question the need to plan in this way, because they think the session is just about showing people some slides and talking through some content. But we want you to have a deeper understanding of what's involved. We encourage you to flip your thinking. It's not about you delivering information, but about how the participants will use it afterwards.

What happens if you don't plan?

It's very easy to find examples of sessions where the person planning it has neglected or forgotten about one of the dimensions. We've all been in sessions where the purpose was unclear, or where people from outside a group, who don't have the right capabilities, have been invited, or where the decision maker isn't present. This all makes it challenging, if not impossible, to have a good-quality session.

Another example of lack of planning is a session where the purpose is to be creative, but the facilitator hasn't prepared for an interactive input session. That means that there is no way to collaborate creatively in a whiteboard platform, such as Miro. As a result, only one person can provide verbal input at a time. That kind of setup isn't conducive to creativity.

Failing to build interaction into sessions is another consequence of not planning properly. If you want people to have ownership of what you're discussing then they need to interact and be part of the process.

Engagement will also be low if participants don't play their parts. For example, if your manager is on the call but isn't actually present. We've often seen the situation where the manager is there but turns their video off, and it's quite obvious that they're sitting there answering emails. The manager might do that because they know what's being shared, but if they don't pay attention then it makes the other participants question why they should place any importance on what's being discussed.

In the next six chapters, we're going to zoom in on each of the points of the Design Star and provide you with practical planning tips and tools. We'll start with a closer look at purpose, which is at the heart of the Star and is what everything else revolves around.

Use the link to find the template for the Design Star as well as examples of the completed form: www.implement.dk/vf#design

7

Purpose

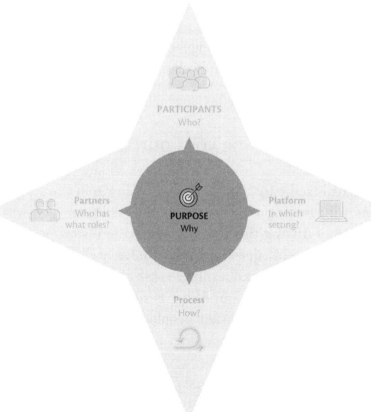

Figure 7.1   Always start with the purpose

The purpose is key to the design of your session. That's why it's at the centre of the Design Star (Figure 7.1). It's the reason for you're meeting. Without a clear purpose it's impossible to have effective sessions; the purpose of the session guides all the other elements of the planning process. Challenge yourself to make the purpose of your session very concrete.

In addition to having a main purpose, you can have sub-purposes for your session. These are things that might not be visible on the agenda but that you believe are a key by-product of the session, such as socialising, building trust or seeing if you are a good match for future collaboration. You should always have one main purpose for the session that is clear to you and your participants and also list any sub-purposes for your session, even if they will not appear on the agenda.

If you don't think about both purposes, you are unlikely to achieve them.

Define your purpose

As a virtual facilitator, your role doesn't begin in the session, it begins with finding the 'Why?'. As the facilitator, you will be in charge of driving this process. The natural starting point is to ask the 'big why' question: Why are we having this session? There are a number of questions to ask alongside this: What is the purpose of the session? What is the impact we might get out of this? Why do we want people to meet? Sometimes the 'Why?' will be very clear, but other times it will require work to define it clearly.

One way to do this is to ask 'Why?' five times. Your initial answer to that question could be, 'To create engagement', but go deeper. Ask why you want to create that engagement, and then ask why again. You want to really dive into the why of this decision until you reach the single most important reason behind the session.

When you are planning a session with other people, the next most important question is: Are we aligned on this 'Why'? Often we find that one person will want one thing, another person will want another thing, and another person will want another thing. They can all have very different 'Whys?' for the session. As the facilitator, it's your job to narrow this down to a common 'Why?'. Sometimes you might need to narrow it down to two 'Whys?' and then wait until the session to choose the 'Why?' that fits with the time.

The most common issues we encounter are that there are too many purposes for a session or that the purpose hasn't been properly considered. If you have too many purposes, you risk not reaching any of them, basically wasting your and other people's time. If you narrow your focus to match time and resources you will see a big impact. If you haven't considered the purpose of a session, you may realise that it's not necessary at all.

Dip into your project management toolbox

This exercise is similar to the one where you're defining the scope or the purpose of a project. In this situation, you also start with the 'Why?'. Make sure the 'Why?' focuses on the effect, not the deliverables. Deliverables are about how you get there, not why you're doing it.

We believe it's essential to start by defining the purpose, before you look at the details, such as how much time you have, how many people you have or what the process should look like. Once you look at the details, you might discover you need to revise the 'Why?', which we'll come to in later chapters. However, it's important that you start with that very clear big ambition and then find a way to make that work within the constraints that you have.

Who defines the purpose?

Who makes the ultimate decision about the 'Why?' for the session will depend on the session or project. Usually it would be the project leader or someone who has something at stake in the session. That might be a group of people or just one person. But at some point, a decision needs to be taken about why you are having that session. Once you've answered the question of the big 'Why?' a good follow-up question to ask is: Once we've conducted this meeting/workshop/session, and it's been a success, what have we achieved? You want to know what you will be talking about afterwards, what you will be standing with in your hands, and what that will look like once you've finished and are really happy. We'll give you some questions to help you define the success criteria of your session in a later subsection of this chapter.

Don't assume everyone knows the purpose

We often see situations where it's taken as a given that people know what the purpose is, but it's really important not to assume that this is the case. Everybody who is part of the design and planning needs to be as certain as you about what you're trying to achieve. This also comes back to what we talked about earlier, about being aligned on your 'Why?'.

How specific do you need to be?

We'll give you some examples at the end of the chapter to illustrate what we would describe as good and specific purposes, but here is a brief example to illustrate what we've talked about so far.

In a business context, a purpose defined as 'everyone getting together' doesn't go deep enough. Instead 'knowledge sharing' could be the purpose of the session, and for everyone in-house to learn about each other's core subject matter expertise, and a sub-purpose of the session would be the social aspect and everyone being together.

A key test to knowing whether you are specific enough in your purpose is working out whether you can evaluate it after the session. If you can look at your purpose and say that you can clearly evaluate it and know what success will look like, then your purpose is specific enough. We believe you need to be able to measure the impact of your session, for example being able to see whether you made a decision about X, Y, Z that everyone believed in.

You also need to be realistic about what can be achieved in the time you have available. One of the biggest challenges we see is that people want to do too much. They start thinking, 'Since we have all the IT people together, it would be nice to fix all these things.' Then they end up with a long list of things that they haven't prioritised. Being specific is important because it allows you to steer your planning back to the main purpose you have defined without getting sidetracked.

Define the success criteria for your session

The next step is to know when your session will be a success. What has to happen during or after the session for you to consider it successful? Be as specific as possible when you are defining these criteria.

We suggest asking yourself questions such as:

- What would need to be true to make this session a success?
- What are the criteria for success?

- What should happen after the session for it to be considered a success?
- What can participants do after the session?

Define your sub-purpose

There are two levels of sub-purpose. One level is the formal sub-purpose, which is something that you could put on the agenda. For example, the purpose of a meeting might be to share progress on the project, while the sub-purpose is to see how you are doing globally on A and B and C.

The other level is the informal sub-purpose. This will often be something intangible, such as wanting everyone in the session to have trust in the way you run the project, or coming across as a decisive person, or even creating high energy among the team before you go on a summer holiday.

As an example, we often have a meeting just before the summer holiday, where the official purpose is to share knowledge, look back on the year that has just passed, look at what we achieved as a team and share some learnings from the past year. That is the official purpose of the meeting and that's what we have on the slide. But the unofficial purpose is to create a high level of energy and pride in the team, so that they leave for their summer holiday with pride and appreciation and want to come back once the summer holiday is over. Often this is the time when people will look for a new job if they're not happy, so we want everyone to leave and want to come back. But we wouldn't put that on a slide. However, if we don't design the session for that energy and pride, it could become a boring knowledge sharing session. Instead, we design it in such a way that everyone on the team feels that they are really proud of what we've achieved.

We also want them to feel as though things are heading in an exciting direction and that they couldn't get similar learnings at another organisation.

Your sub-purpose can help you to specify the overall purpose of the session, but it's important to strike the right balance between your main purpose and your sub-purpose(s). There's a fine balance between these formal and informal purposes, and you need to make sure that a session doesn't become manipulative because you've stated that it's got one formal purpose, but really you're focusing on an informal purpose.

Refining many purposes into one

While some people may not have any purpose, or may not know what their purpose is, others have the opposite problem in that they have big ambitions and too many purposes for a single session.

As an example, we met with a client recently who told us he wanted to talk about his liquidity, omni-channels, planning and also how weak he found his leadership role. He wanted to talk about all of this in the scope of maybe three or four meetings. While this is an extreme example, we often encounter people who have many ambitions and want to achieve many things. In this instance, as a facilitator, your job is to help them prioritise what is important and what to deal with first. For this particular client, we gave him our advice about where to start and then gave him a high-level view of the process to show how to move forward and get the desired effect.

Sometimes it may be logical to have two different meetings instead of one if there are lots of different groups involved and people with different backgrounds, aspirations or expectations.

This all comes back to impact, alongside solving your purpose. If you want to have an impact and solve your purpose, you can't do it all at once. You need to slice it up and go for maybe a smaller impact but one that achieves your purpose, instead of trying to grasp it all and end up not coming away with any of it.

Examples of specific purposes

- To launch the new global strategy and create energy about the new direction for the company.
- Connect the leadership team even tighter together through an open dialogue about the learning from collaboration in the past couple of months.
- Create a number of new ideas on how to work more efficiently, and virtually, together in the project team.
- To create daily alignment of tasks in the team.
- Inspire people with new ways of working.

8

Participants

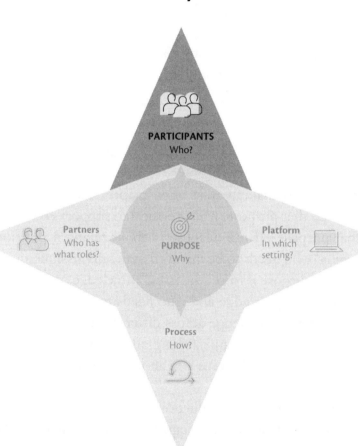

Figure 8.1 Who are the right people for the session?

Bring the right people into your session to ensure you can make the decisions according to your purpose (Figure 8.1). But don't bring everyone – only ask the ones you need to succeed with your purpose. Also it's important to be aware of who's present in the session to be able to design a good process for them. In essence, it's not about getting a lot of people in the room, it's about getting the right people in the room who will support the purpose.

All too often, we see sessions where the organiser just hasn't thought about it. They've invited people from a staple list, rather than creating a contributor list. If you're inviting participants from a staple list then we suggest you revisit the purpose to make sure it's the right one for your session. At this stage you could consider stakeholder mapping to decide who should actually participate.

Who should participate?

Before you start making a list of participants, look at your purpose. Given that purpose, who is critical to support you in reaching that purpose? If the purpose is about taking a position on something, who needs to be involved in the discussions and decision? If the purpose is to get the latest knowledge on a topic, who will share that knowledge and who needs to hear it? If the purpose is to share knowledge across different teams, is it relevant to everyone in every team? Asking and answering these kinds of questions will usually give you an idea of who needs to be in the session.

As we said in the introduction to Part II, sometimes you'll be in a scenario where the participants are already decided. If you cannot choose for yourself who is going to be in the session, then we recommend you go back and revisit whether the purpose you have is a fitting purpose for that group of people. Often we find there isn't enough challenge about who the participants should be. You have to be more strategic, prioritise and place a greater focus on the key people in the session, whether you need the right subject matter expertise, the right decision-making power or the right experience and abilities in the session. Don't just invite the usual suspects.

Contribution vs attendance

When you are deciding who should participate, this isn't just about who should attend. It's about who can and should contribute, as well as about anyone who might need to be there to receive information. Who needs to do something afterwards to achieve the impact that you've defined in your purpose? Think about who you need to have to help you get there. That might mean you need someone in a leadership role to be part of your session, not as contributors in the session itself, but for their role in driving a behaviour change afterwards.

Less is more

It's very easy to add participants to virtual sessions. It's nothing more than a click. But what we often see is that when you scale up a virtual room, people are less likely to engage in it. The difference between having three or four people in a session compared to eight is tremendous and has a big impact in the sense of how much speaking time you all have and how you interact.

For instance, when you have more than five or six people in a virtual meeting, everyone needs to be muted, which can create a barrier to talking. By contrast, if you have three or four people in a virtual meeting, everyone can have their microphones unmuted and you'll find there's a rhythm of speaking more freely. That's not to say it can't work that way with larger groups too, but it's another aspect of the dynamic that you need to be aware of. We recommend carefully considering what you gain and what you lose in terms of inviting or not inviting additional participants to your session.

Know who will be in the virtual space

Once you have your target list of participants, think about who they are in greater detail. We suggest questions such as:

- Are they managers, employees, engineers or technical experts?
- Are the participants choosing to be there?
- Are they more senior participants?
- Are they digital natives?
- Are participants coming from different departments?
- Do they have different cultures?
- Is there any history between them, or between you and your participants, that it is important to bear in mind?

It's important to have an accurate mental image of who they are in order to design a session with impact and engagement.

The reason that we often go to participants after discussing purpose is because knowing who your participants are can influence other parts of your Design Star. Once you know more about who will be in your session, you can use that understanding to help you choose the platform and design the process to engage them.

You can also consider whether there are any participants who will only need to be there for one part of the session, not its entirety. We'll cover this in greater detail in Chapter 10 when we look at specific parts and roles within sessions.

Understanding your participants

The other angle to this is that getting to know your participants can help you understand their thought processes and natural preferences. Some will have a natural preference for facts, details and data. Others will be more prone to thinking about the mood and people participating. Then you have the visionary or creative approach. We recommend that you think about the preferences of your participants and plan to either match or challenge them according to your purpose. Often you can host a session that's in line with your own thinking patterns and preferences, but that doesn't necessarily cater for those in the session who have another thinking pattern or preference.

You could also consider how you expect your participants to feel about the subject or topic that you'll be discussing. Do they have any prior knowledge or assumptions about it? Do they like the topic or are there some negative barriers surrounding it that you'll need to address? This crosses over with the platform element of planning and what mindset you want them to be in when they join the session.

It's also important to be aware of the tech skills of your participants because this will affect how you design your session. If you know that they are all comfortable with a particular platform, you might choose to use that for the entire session. Or if you know they have good tech skills and are virtually competent, you might consider sending them out to other platforms. Or if you want to use other platforms but don't feel that all the participants will be comfortable, then you need to consider how you can build their competency ahead of the session.

The overall purpose of this part of the Design Star is to make sure you have the right people in your session and that you design with these participants in mind. To do this effectively, consider everything – from what time of day you're holding the session to the mental state your participants will be coming in with. Are they young digital natives, or are they people who are less skilled with IT? Are they more data driven or more people driven? It's important to have an accurate mental image of who they are. You also need to be aware of any different dynamics within the group and think about whether there are any dynamics, cultures or histories that you need to take into account when you're designing your session.

9

Platform

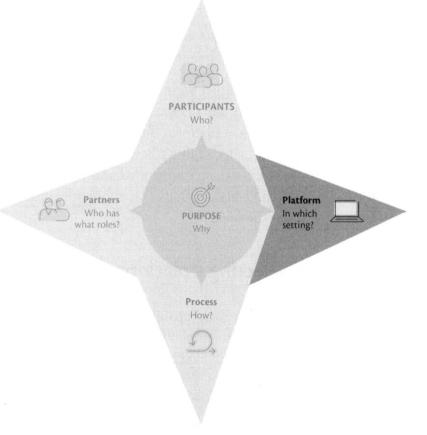

Figure 9.1   Consider the platform and the setting

In a virtual session you aren't all physically in the same place, but you use a platform, such as Zoom or Teams, to host a session. However, the platform isn't just the technology you use (Figure 9.1). It's also the physical platform, or environment, that you and your participants are situated in. We advise that you make sure that you are in a physical location supporting the session and also encourage your participants to do the same. Finally, we recommend that you help the participants get into the right mindset for your session. It's another aspect of the platform you're creating. We'll dive into mindset in more detail in the next chapter though.

The tech platform is crucial to hosting a virtual session, so make sure you have one that supports your session and you know how to use it. Having said that, way too often we see people taking too much time and energy to research and select the 'perfect' platform.

We recommend you direct your energy towards designing your session and mastering the chosen platform. In our experience, it's always best to use a platform that you already have and already know, if possible. If you don't have a platform that you use already, choose one that's recommended and that you know works. Remember that virtual facilitation is about humans creating results, not about the tech.

Selecting a platform

As well as considering your own capabilities and existing skills as a facilitator, you also need to think about your participants and their tech skills. The platform you choose for your session will depend on them as well as on you. Consider what they might be used to. Be aware of the entry barriers that we discussed in Chapter 4. Remember that a session that you've designed to be really cool will be the opposite if your participants can't join or don't know how to use the platform.

Although selecting the right platform is important, we would say that *how* you use your chosen platform is more important than the specific platform that you choose. There are many ways to use any given platform and there are processes that allow you to do more than you might imagine. Therefore this choice often comes back to the skills, capacity and creativity of the facilitator and participants rather than the constraints of the platform.

When you're thinking about the capabilities of the participants, start by asking if there is one platform that is already in use at your organisation. As the facilitator, it is much easier for you to learn to use one new tool than to ask multiple participants to learn to use a new tool. It's about keeping the entry barrier as low as possible for your participants.

Remember that often we aren't talking about just using one platform. In many cases, we would recommend that you use multiple platforms. This means you're not constrained by the main one that you're using, because you can combine this with other platforms and tools to enable different ways of collaborating during your session. You should always come back to your purpose and make sure that the platform or platforms you've chosen support the purpose of the session.

There are endless numbers of platforms available. Some are for communication, some are for collaboration and file sharing and others are for interactions. This tech is always evolving. We already covered this in Chapter 4, and below are a few examples of some of the platforms we use at Implement Consulting Group at the time of writing.

- Communication: Zoom, Teams, Hangout
- Collaboration/file sharing: Howspace, Miro, Padlet
- Interactions: Menti, Kahoot

For comparisons of some of the different tools you can use, tap in to our online resources. www.implement.dk/vf#tech

Top tip: Use what you have and can already use

If you already have a platform (it could be Teams), all participants have an account, you know it works with your VPN and people know how to attend a workshop using that platform, then it makes sense to stick with that, even if you know there might be another tool out there that may be slightly better for the precise kind of workshop you're planning.

There are several reasons for this. Firstly, as the facilitator, if you need to learn to use a new platform to the level where you can facilitate a virtual session, it may take you a lot of time and effort best used for other activities. Secondly, this will also apply to the participants. Don't make them learn something new if you don't have to. Thirdly, if you try to introduce a new tool you'll not only need to spend time educating yourself about how to use it, but also educating others.

To start using a completely new platform, the features that it provides should be much greater for your purpose than the one you already have and know.

Questions to help you select the right platform

To make sure that you choose your platform with your participants and purpose in mind, ask yourself the following questions:

1. As the facilitator, what can I use?
2. What do the participants know how to use?
3. How tech mature are my participants?
4. How many different platforms/switches can they handle?

For example, you could design a very interactive session where you take them back and forth between many different platforms, or you could design a steady session where you stay mainly on one platform. If your participants will struggle to navigate their way back from a new platform to the one you started on, you would consider designing a steady session.

Figure 9.2 shows three circles representing your competence or capabilities with regards to platform(s) as a facilitator, the participants' competence and capabilities, and the purpose of the session. Start looking at the overlap between participants

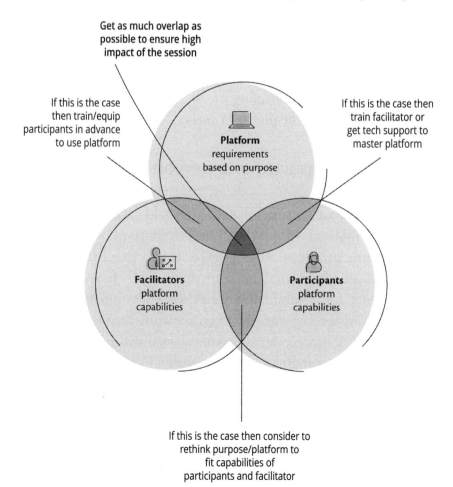

Figure 9.2   Ensure overlap between capabilities and platform(s)

and purpose to see if you have a platform that could be used. Hopefully you are also capable of using this platform. If there is an overlap between the capabilities of the participants and the platform that supports the purpose and you aren't capable as a facilitator, then it's your responsibility to make sure you overlap with the other two circles or you find someone to help you bridge that gap. The most important part is that there's an overlap between the participants and the platform that supports the purpose of the session.

This doesn't mean you should never use a platform that your participants haven't tried before, but if you decide to do this then it is your responsibility to train them briefly in how to use that platform. We've seen many examples of this working incredibly well, but you have to be aware that you will need to spend some time before or at the beginning of the session giving them some guidance about how the platform works.

Always stipulate one person per device

Tell all of your participants that they should each join your virtual session on their own device. This is important because if you have multiple people sharing a device it will affect their ability to interact and fully participate in the session. If you want to do breakouts, for example, this won't work if you have multiple people sharing a computer. Or if you are using the chat function, having multiple people on the same device will mean that not everyone can contribute or read the chat.

As well as making sure that each participant has their own device, we usually recommend that you specify that each person should have a device where they can see and write. This is the kind of information you send out before your session as part of the preparation.

Don't forget the physical

Even though we are participating in a session virtually, we all have to sit somewhere in the physical world. While you can't set up everyone's physical environment for them, you can provide them with guidance about how to set up their physical platform so that they are able to get the most out of your session. Invite them to arrange themselves in a specific way, and provide advice on how to do this to get the most out of the platform you'll be using. Think about all the components we discussed in the tech chapter – a quiet room, steady video connection, a light from behind the screen, having water, coffee and snacks to hand. Encourage people to create a pleasant physical environment for themselves that will mean they are able to engage in the session in a nice way and keep their focus. We always send an invitation mail including tips and tricks for this to remind participants, as illustrated in Chapter 4.

You could also consider sending your participants some-thing physical to accompany the session. That might be a booklet for use during the session, or it could be drinks to have together after the session to celebrate. If you decide to do this, ensure that you make arrangements in good time so that everyone will have the physical element you are sending. Don't forget to plan time for lunch into your session too and think about how all the par-ticipants may use that time.

Within an office environment, this may also mean thinking about how you can rearrange the space to make sure that people have somewhere to go, where they can be free of disturbance dur-ing a virtual session without needing to occupy an entire meeting room. A phone booth or discreet cubicle might be suitable.

10

Process

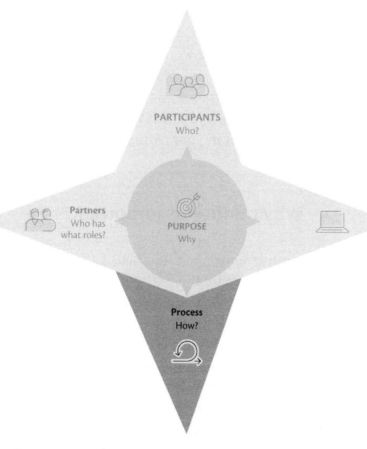

Figure 10.1   Select and design the right process for the session

The process is the very way the session is framed and conducted and depends on the purpose of the session, as well as on the other points of the Design Star (Figure 10.1). We would encourage you to be creative! The process spans the before and during stages. There are even elements that carry over into the period after a session too.

In the before phase you're designing a specific process planning what will actually happen – with information, exercises and interaction – but also invitation, prework and even what to do after the session. This is both to have a practical plan and to create the right mindset for participants before they join the session. Will it have a high level of engagement or will it be more of a presentation? Will you have breakouts and collaborative working documents? Will there be work for participants before and after the session? What you want to find is the type of process that will best serve your purpose.

The first part of the process that we're going to explore is creating the right mindset in your participants in the lead-up to your session.

Why mindset is important

In Chapter 8 we mentioned the mindset of your participants, making sure that you prepare them to join your session with the right mindset to get the most out of the session.

It's important that all your participants come into your session with clear expectations that are in line with your purpose. There are a number of things you can do before a session to set those expectations – from sending invitations, to setting pre-work to be completed in preparation for the session.

What you want to avoid is having to spend the first 10 to 20 minutes of your session getting all your participants on the same page in terms of mindset. Think about how you can make sure that they are ready and mentally in the right place from the first minute of your virtual session.

How can you create the right mindset?

If you think about it in the context of physical sessions, the setting you would choose for your session says a lot about what mindset you expect people to have. If you are invited to a workshop that is being hosted at a hotel, you're likely to approach that differently to a workshop being hosted in the basement meeting room that you use all the time. In the virtual world you don't have that physical setting to influence the participants' mindsets, and getting another invite for a Teams workshop isn't likely to do a lot for their mindset. This means you need to look for different ways that you can make them curious, or energetic, or ready for learning right from the very start of your session.

Begin by thinking about the invites you're sending out for your session. A standard Zoom invite, for example, has lots of numbers in it and can be confusing and not very motivating. We've seen examples where people create invitations where they explain a little about the session and send out the link, which sets some expectations and starts to prepare the participants' mindsets, just with the invite. Or you might consider including a link to a movie or trailer that sets the tone for the session.

Another way to create the right mindset is to let participants do some work before the session. It could be to read an article, take a test or interview three customers about the theme of the session. Anything that helps them think about what you're going to talk about. Be creative! Make sure it's clear that participants are expected to do this. Asking them to send the results of their preparatory work to you (e.g. key points from the interviews) can be an effective way to ensure it is done.

Use the link to access a blog with three examples of preparation tasks. www.implement.dk/vf#methods

Your aim should be to make people curious about your session and to help them to look forward to it. This comes back to the concept that if you want to facilitate good virtual sessions, you need to direct your energy towards the participants before you enter the session.

What kind of session serves my purpose?

When you decide on the process during the session, consider what kind of session will best suit your purpose. In Chapter 2 we introduced the Five Levels of Involvement: Telling, Selling, Testing, Training and Co-creating.

Selling and telling meetings, for example, would typically be presentations and primarily involve one-way communication (PowerPoint, speaking with notes, lecturing in form of a flip chart with key pointers). There might be a little bit of Q&A, so the process for these kinds of meetings would be a one-way street for communication, or one where there is a limited period of two-way communication. The key is that there is a firm solution that you arrive at with your process. Training also falls into this category because there's a right and a wrong outcome; there's a particular solution or outcome and that requires a certain process to get you there. Yet when we talk about training, there is likely to be much more interaction.

In terms of testing or co-creating, this will be more of an open discussion about something. There will be much more communication between the facilitator and the participants, and there won't be a right or wrong outcome from that kind of session. Here it is often about finding a common solution, producing ideas, collecting insights, improving a prototype etc. through different ways of interacting.

When you are designing the process for the session, always ask yourself: What is the purpose? Do I want an open discussion? Am I looking for a decision? Am I sharing information?

Set your corner flags

We mentioned setting corner flags earlier in the book and this is an important model to consider when you're designing the process. When you are designing your process look at your corner flags, decide what is open for discussion in the session and what is not, so that not only you as the facilitator, but also the participants, clearly know the boundaries within the session. Once you have those in place, you can design the process based on what is open for discussion.

Where are you in the decision house?

If you are facilitating a process towards a decision it can be helpful to be very clear during the design phase on when you are going to explore and open the topic, gather input and are trying to understand it. That's where you start. Imagine that this is the first floor of your house. You've stepped inside the topic but you're not ready to make a decision yet.

At some stage, you will be ready to climb the stairs to the second floor of the house. This will be at the point that you feel you have sufficient knowledge about the topic, and that you've received input from the right people to be ready to move towards a decision. You're closing down the discussion and not taking new input. That's when you make a decision, when you're on the second floor of the decision house. Designing processes for decision-making should include both 'floors' in the same session or deliberately designed into different sessions.

Examples of different processes

There are many examples of good processes you can use to facilitate virtual sessions. In the table below and in the cases later in the book you'll find suggestions. Don't forget you can always make up your own. There are many more in our online resources, where we go into more detail about how to use different process methods. www.implement.dk/vf#methods

---

'The producer'

Purpose of the process: Get inputs from participants to qualify a solution.

Platforms and materials: Create breakout rooms for your groups and a shared PowerPoint template with nice visuals and clear instructions, and boxes ready to add notes into.

Process:

1. Instruct participants about the exercise, the why, how the inputs will be used and what is expected in plenary. Each group should work on inputs for one area.

   • Be clear with your instructions and visualise them.

   • Ask the groups to assign a timekeeper and someone to ensure that they document their discussions.

2. Provide participants with links for a shared document such as PowerPoint. In PowerPoint place the instructions on each slide and make sure that group numbers are visual.

3. Send them out in breakout rooms and give them time to work.

4. Go visit the breakout rooms to check that the task is understood and they remember to document. Remember to let them know that you are there!

5. Bring the participants back to plenary and assign someone responsible for commenting. Go through each slide sharing your screen, letting the groups explain what they suggested. Ask if any else has comments and make sure to add these on the slides.

6. Wrap up the process by explaining how you'll use the inputs going forward.

Examples of processes to encourage engagement

Below are the main examples of processes you could introduce into your session to encourage engagement and social relations among the participants (Figure 10.2).

You may want to use all of them or just some of them. We would advise, however, that the longer your session is the more of these you will want to use.

Virtual processes are not that different from physical ones. Sometimes you simply need to translate what you would have done physically into a virtual setting and think about what opportunities you have to do that in a virtual space. Below we present some of our process methods for inspiration that we use in many different sessions to create process-oriented involvement.

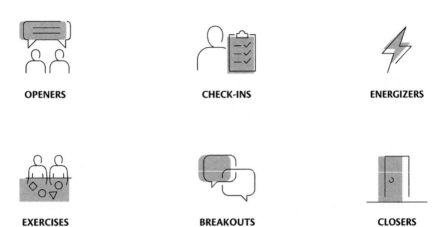

Figure 10.2   Processes to encourage engagement

Openers

Think of this as a can opener. You want to make sure that all the participants feel like they are part of the session and not just passive listeners. Getting everyone to contribute within the first ten minutes of the session is a great start for this. With openers, the purpose is to engage all the participants, not just one, and make them feel like they are part of the session. Introduce who is in the room. You might make a suggestion, such as, 'Introduce yourself and say where you are located' or ask a question, like 'What do you hope to get out of this session?' or 'What is one thing that's on your mind right now?'. Whatever it is, it should be an open question. If there are more than seven of you in a session, it's best to do this in a breakout session to create a sense of intimacy, or use the chat or annotations features.

You can also use your opener to get the participants into the right mindset for the session. One aspect of this process is engagement and the other is focusing people's minds on the topic that you will be talking about.

Check-ins

A check-in is a short ongoing interaction throughout the session where you are checking in with the group and where they are right now on each topic. It's an opportunity for the participants to give feedback on the process or content. It's also a chance for you to ask if they have any questions, how they feel about the session so far and where their energy levels are. We recommend having a check-in every ten minutes during plenary sessions. You could ask people in the chat, use the small participant engagement such as raise hand or "ok", or via a poll. These check-ins can give you a hint whether you should proceed, take a break, or introduce an energiser.

Short check-ins are especially important in a virtual setting because it's more difficult to know how people feel in a virtual session. Facilitators often tell us that they struggle to feel the participants because they can't see them or only their faces and they feel like they're talking to an empty screen. This is why check-ins are so important. As the facilitator, it's your job to engage participants and get this feedback to help you read the room.

Energisers

Energisers are often forgotten in a virtual setting, even though many people actually need, like and use energisers in physical sessions. The purpose of virtual energisers is to engage the group. They are about regaining energy, or making sure that participants are in the right state to move on. Usually this involves something physical or touching on the emotions. It can be through fun and humour, introducing a competition, getting people to wonder about something or getting them to move physically. When we talk about energisers we can consider five different types depending on what you want to accomplish.

- Social energisers – to bring the group closer emotionally.
- Funny energisers – to make people laugh and to defocus for a short while.
- Focus energisers – to focus energy for difficult or deep work.
- Competitions – to raise energy and test knowledge.
- Physical exercises – to make people move and get some fresh air to the brain.

You need to get a little bit creative in terms of what you do. Here are just a few examples of energisers to get you thinking.

- Get everyone to stand up and do a two-minute squat exercise ('Bring Sally Up' provides great musical support for this, moving up when they sing up, and down when they sing down).
- Guide participants through some stretching or breathing for one minute.
- Do a short music quiz with 3–4 questions.
- Do a drawing exercise on the whiteboard.
- Get people to try to solve a puzzle.
- Do a one-minute plank together.
- Start a 'speed dating' exercise where people discuss something funny that they've done.

Look through the online resources to find specific exercises to use regarding process methods in virtual facilitation. www.implement.dk/vf#methods

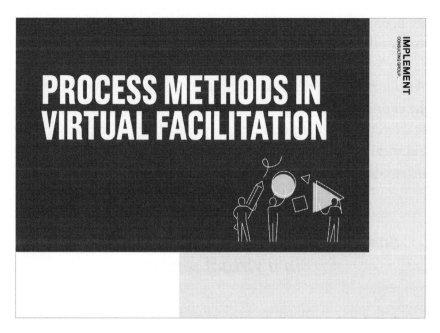

Source: Implement Consulting Group

Exercises and processes

When we talk about virtual exercises and processes, we are talking about actually producing some kind of concrete output, whether that's having a discussion that leads to some kind of output on a whiteboard or in a shared document, or getting the group to come back with ideas. When we your purpose and make sure people are engaged the whole way through. Your job is to get people to work and produce some kind of output, and to let that happen, whether you're giving them individual work, setting up breakout sessions or working in plenary. We'll provide you with some examples of how to introduce exercises during virtual sessions in Chapter 17.

When you are planning exercises, think about how you will guide people through them and maintain the energy and involvement throughout. Also take advantage of the virtual format to get people to contribute in shared documents during the session so it's easy to share results afterwards. It can also be useful to have a list of exercises and energisers that aren't necessarily part of your plan, but that you could use on the day if you find that the energy is dropping or you find a different need. These should be exercises or energisers that you don't have to prepare from a technical perspective, but that you can introduce if you feel they are needed during the session.

Some suggestions for getting into exercises in a virtual session

- Let people think for 30 seconds for themselves before they share their thoughts in plenary and open up the discussion.

- Discuss the topic by interviewing a panel of different experts or users.

- Get people to draw on a whiteboard where everyone is chipping in with their ideas, and sorting and grouping them as they go.

- Work in smaller groups in shared documents on a specific task and present in plenary.

- Present content in plenary and have participants evaluate it using specific criteria in breakrooms before they come back into plenary.

Find suggestions for virtual process methods in our online resources. www.implement.dk/vf#methods

Breakout rooms

Breakout rooms are used to create smaller spaces for each participant to discuss a subject, do some efficient work in smaller groups, give feedback to one another, and so on. It's a great way to create focus and engagement during virtual sessions and a huge 'virtual' advantage: it's easy to switch between plenary and breakouts and you don't need ten minutes every time you switch, because people don't have to move physically, or see it as an opening to run to the bathroom or the coffee machine.

Breakout rooms present a good opportunity for the facilitator to create a safe space for discussion, and it's easier to ask for input when people are back in the main session when you know that they have already had the chance to discuss the question. You can ask, 'What did you talk about?' or 'What did you and your partners discuss?'. This makes it easier for people to be open, because they can share their thoughts having already tested their perspective in a smaller setting. It creates psychological safety in your meeting and it means you're not singling out one person and asking for their opinion without giving them a chance to think about it properly.

When you're setting up breakouts it's really important to let people know what's expected of them. Don't ask them to do multiple things, just give them one assignment and make sure the instructions are written in the shared document or platform if people use these during breakouts. If you have more instructions, save them and call people back when it's time for them to move onto something else. It's also important to use timeboxing, especially when you use breakouts, because it's hard for people to know when to come back.

The bigger your sessions get, the harder it is for participants to feel as though they can say something. One way of addressing this is to use breakout rooms and to ask each group to choose a spokesperson who will be responsible for coming back from the breakout and telling the rest of the participants what you talked about. This means that person will have the acceptance for speaking on behalf of the whole group.

See Figure 10.3 for a summary of ideas for involving participants in your session.

OPENERS

- What are your expectations? (Open answer in menti.com)
- What do I already know about ...? (Word cloud in menti.com)
- Level of pre-understanding of the topic (Quiz, Brainstorm,)
- Share the highlight of your day / weekend

CHECK-INS

- What is your energy level right now? (Poll)
- What questions do you have about this? (Q&A)
- How comfortable are you in this area? (Poll)
- What do you need? (Whiteboard)

ENERGIZERS

- Stretching
- Sketching
- Quiz
- Brain breaks
- Drawing
- Physical mini-workout

EXERCISES

- Individual reflections (Think first – Share in plenary)
- Create & share ideas (Draw on whiteboard)
- Sorting and grouping ideas (Moving objects)
- Identify gap / challenges (Fill in template)
- Evaluate content or self-assessment (Polls)
- Vote for solutions (Poll)
- Call and talk in pairs

BREAKOUT ROOMS

- How can you use/apply this? (Discussion)
- Create a plan and how to use it at your place (Commitment)
- Come up with 3 suggestions! (Crow solving)
- What do you think about it? (Social reflection)
- What have you learned until now? (Teach-back)
- What questions do you have now? (Create psychological)

CLOSERS

- What did you learn from this session?
- What is your next step?
- What is your level of understanding of the learning objective?
- Feedback on this session

Figure 10.3   Summary of some different ideas to foster involvement

Design your process, then your slides

Once you have decided on the process you will use during your session and you have described how this will look at a high level, you can translate this into the slides or whatever materials and resources you need to present it. That could be in the form of a shared PowerPoint, Howspace or any other platform you choose. The idea is that you take your process and translate it into something that's tangible that you can use on the day.

Design the before phase and follow-up too

Think about the process before and after the session as well. This is very important to ensure maximum impact of your session. Could you make your participants more ready with a preparation task, so you can produce a better result during the session? Could you ensure that impact by looking not only at the session, but also at what happens afterwards? If you haven't thought about what will happen afterwards, in terms of who will use the inputs that come out of the session or whom a decision needs to be shared with, then information could be lost and you won't create the right impact with your session or deliver the right outcomes. It comes back to the old idea that you start with the end.

11

Partners

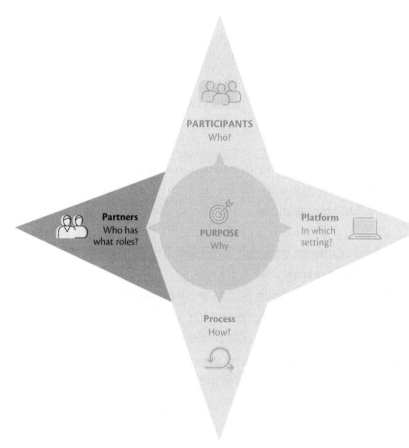

Figure 11.1   Partners for the session

Clearly defined partners are key to ensure a smooth flow during your session, getting the right input from the right people at the right time (Figure 11.1). There will be people in your session who play a crucial part in achieving the purpose of the session. We already touched upon the different roles in your session. There will obviously be a facilitator for the main session. You may also want a facilitator for breakout sessions, if you're running any, or assign participants to do this. It might be that you need input from key experts. Or that you need a leader to be present to make a key decision or address something specific. You should also consider whether you need a technical assistant to take care of the logistical side of the session. The aim with this final point of the Design Star is to think about who will stand out in terms of making the session a success. These are your partners.

Also think about what parts you need to play in order to achieve the purpose of the session. Do you need to be a challenger or a supporter?

Are you there facilitating or do you also play a part as an expert? We often ask our clients how they want us to be as the facilitator. Do they want us to be the challenger or do they want us to act as the person who is seeking all the different perspectives to find common ground? Is it okay for us to challenge them in front of their team?

Once you know which parts you need people to play in your session, you need to make sure that you're aligned with your partners who have a crucial role in the session. Make sure they're prepared, both physically in terms of having their slides ready, and mentally in terms of showing up with the right mindset knowing their part.

These are the two essential questions to ask in order to define and then align:

1. What partners do we need to make this session a success?
2. Are we in accordance or alignment about how we act out those roles?

For example, the decision maker might be a clearly defined role, but have you agreed exactly how you will make decisions in the session or how that person will present themselves to the other participants in the session? It's the same if you're the facilitator. The role itself is clearly defined, but there are many ways in which you can fulfil that role, so you should decide before the session how you will do this to best support the purpose.

What parts does the facilitator play?

As the facilitator you need to think carefully about all the parts you will need to play in a session. You may need to step in and out of several roles during a session. You might be invited in as an expert to share your insights or advice, or you could be asked to take a stand at certain points and at other times facilitate what is happening in the session. You might also need to train participants in how to use a new tool. Remember that it can be difficult to wear many different hats.

The clearer you know the roles you'll need to play, the easier it is to say to the participants in your session that your role is changing. For example, you might say, 'I'm going from being the facilitator to being the expert for ten minutes,' and once you've delivered your insight, you say, 'So, given that insight, what do you think?' With those two sentences bookending your insight, you've seamlessly switched from facilitator to expert and back again.

The parts you might need to play during a session as a facilitator

- Engagement facilitator
- Challenger
- Trainer
- Expert
- Producer
- Tech support
- Decision maker

Think about what else may need to change to signal to the participants that you're changing roles. Do you need to alter your body language, if they can see you on their screens, or will your tone of voice change? Can you make a physical gesture to indicate that you're stepping into a new role, almost like changing your hat?

In a physical setting you might physically move to another place in the room, but in a virtual setting this is more challenging. This is particularly important in smaller sessions because it's in these scenarios that you're likely to be playing multiple roles as the facilitator. In larger sessions, you are much more likely to have a separate producer, call in an expert and so on, allowing you to focus more on simply being the facilitator.

When you are changing roles, it's vital that you communicate this to the other participants in the session. You need to be clear on which part you're playing and so should everyone else. It comes back to the concept we talked about earlier in the book: you need to know which dance you're dancing and the participants need to know which dance they're watching. If you don't clearly communicate this, you can leave people feeling confused, which can affect engagement and progress towards your purpose.

Do other people need to change parts?

Not everyone will need to play the same part for the duration of the session. For example, you might have people who are in the session purely as participants. But you may have other participants who, at some point during the session, will need to become a partner. They might be a subject area expert, for instance, or be the key decision maker. You may have other partners who aren't participants during the session, but who will be needed to fulfil a role for just part of the session, like an expert giving a presentation or sharing their insights with the rest of the participants.

If you have participants who will need to switch to playing a new part during the session, you, as the facilitator, have to consider how you can manage that and help them understand their changing roles. In a physical environment, you might tap someone on the shoulder to remind them that they'll be playing an important role in the next part of the agenda, or to indicate that you'd like them to share their insights with the rest of the room.

In the virtual world, you'll use other cues so that a participant knows when they will be expected to swap roles or step in and deliver their contribution.

Do you need experts?

One of the great things about virtual sessions is that it's considerably easier to bring in experts from geographically different locations. The world has definitely become smaller in that sense. You could bring in an expert from the US, Denmark, or anywhere in the world if you wanted to, much more easily than if you were in a physical setting.

Do you need breakout room facilitators?

Breakout room facilitators are very helpful if you decide that you want to include breakout rooms in your session. In our experience, people often shy away from using virtual breakout rooms because they are concerned about how they will manage the breakout rooms from a technical perspective.

Introducing breakout room facilitators can help remove this barrier. They can keep track of time, make sure everyone in each breakout room is getting involved, ensure everyone is following the guidelines for this part of the session, answer questions and communicate with the lead facilitator.

Preparing these partners for their role in advance is important. You may even want to do a dry run to ensure you know how the tech works and feel confident in not only using the tools to facilitate breakout rooms, but also in running them.

Invisible partners

There are also what we would describe as invisible partners. This might be where you prep one of the participants to ask the first question in a Q&A session, for instance, to get the questions to start flowing. The idea is that no one else knows that you've pre-arranged this, but that person still has a role to play and it's important for facilitating that part of the session.

How long does each part last?

Remember that not everyone involved in your session will need to be there for its entirety. You may only need an expert to make a contribution during one part of your session, for instance. They may not need to stay in the session beyond that. This is about using everyone's time efficiently.

12

Planning the Session

O nce you have worked through all the points of the Design
Star, you are ready to move to the next steps of the planning process. In this chapter we'll provide you with an overview
of how to work your way through the Design Star and explore
the next steps – setting the agenda, creating a playbook and the
materials for your session.

Using the Design Star in practice

The work with the Design Star can be an individual task but we
encourage you to do it together with the planning team and/or
your 'customer' since it creates clarity and sets the direction for
the following design work.

How-to guide: The Design Star

1. Use a Miro board of the Design Star or draw the star on a flipchart/A3 print of the template depending on the setting for your working session. For each of the following steps one or more members of the group take notes in Miro or notes on Post-its and place them according to what's being discussed.

2. Start with the centre of the star: **The purpose**

   a. Question 'upwards' to define the purpose: 'What is the objective of this session?', 'What is the session meant to contribute to?', 'Why are we having the session?', 'When we have succeeded with a great session what have we achieved?'.

   b. Question 'downwards' to define the deliverables: 'What should we have when the session is finished?' 'What should we have produced?'.

3. **Participants**: 'Who are the "right" people for this process and the purpose of the process?', 'Who can qualify the content, and who can take decisions?'; if this dimension is 'locked', ask: 'Who are the participants?', 'What background do they have?', 'What are their preferences?', 'What is their relative seniority, and their relationship to each other; what organisation and power balance is there between the participants?', 'What is their virtual maturity level?'.

4. **Platform**: 'What is the right technological platform to support the purpose?', 'How can we create the right

physical and psychological platform to match the objective of the process?', 'Are the participants capable of contributing technically and mentally?', 'What equipment should be used to run the session?'; if this dimension is 'locked', ask: 'Are there ways to cope with the technical platform that is given?', 'Can we do something about the physical or mental platform?' (ex. not have the majority in one room and the rest on mobile devices).

5. **Process**: 'What process method(s) should be used during the session?', 'How can we establish the right flow to achieve the objective?', 'What methods (openers, closers, energisers) can we use to generate the right energy and mood?', 'Is there anything to bear in mind with regard to breaks in the course of the session?'.

6. **Partners**: 'Who plays what role on the day?', 'What are the roles of the facilitator, the chair, the technical support, project leader and the presenter?', 'How do we handle/give signals?', 'How do we handle transitions?', 'How do we help each other to do the best possible job?'.

7. It will often be natural to draw up a rough outline of the **programme** with the main agenda items for the day immediately after working on the Design Star, but without going into detail just yet. After this session, you can transfer a fair copy of the Design Star to the playbook template and start to develop the playbook itself.

Use the link to find our Design Star template for download or as a virtual collaboration tool in Miro. www.implement. dk/vf#design

Creating your agenda and playbook

Once you have this overview, where you've agreed upon the purpose, participants, platform, process and partners, you're in a position to begin zooming in on the specific flow of the session, creating the agenda and your playbook for the session (Figure 12.1). We use the agenda as a high-level description of the elements and progress in the session shared with participants prior and during the session, where the playbook is the very specific plan for the facilitator and perhaps others playing a part.

Start looking at your purpose and your initial thoughts about the process and use this to create an agenda defining the main steps in the session to reach your purpose. The agenda is a good place to start to decide on the overall progress of the session. The agenda should provide an overview of the themes or activities during the session. Think of how you name the different steps, as this will affect the mindset of the participants. If you

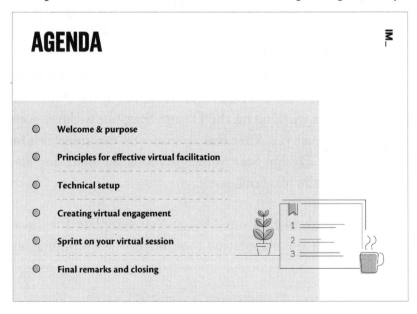

Figure 12.1   A sample agenda
Source: Implement Consulting Group

can do an agenda that motivates people to join your session, it's a good start (as long as it is in accordance with the actual content in the session). Also consider how specific the agenda needs to be – do you want to name the overall themes or do you want to illustrate the entire process? Some people like it to be very specific, others prefer a more high-level overview. The more specific you make it, the less flexible you get. We also often don't add timing to the agenda (but keep it in the playbook), to stay flexible during the session, but sometimes participants with certain preferences like it. It's up to you to decide. Finally we recommend you share it with participants, as a part of the invitation, to set their expectations.

Example of agenda for 2.5 hours: Workshop about personal energy management from 09.00–11.30

- The room opens 15 minutes prior to the session for informal check-in
- Welcome & purpose
- Program and tech
- Introduction to energy
- Physical energy
- Mental energy
- Emotional energy
- Spiritual energy
- 30-day mission
- Landing: Final remarks and closing

When you have decided on your agenda it's time to move on to the playbook. This is where you add the overall process steps from the agenda and specify who will do it and how it will be executed. If you are not specific on the process yet, now is the time to decide.

We use the template in Figure 12.2 to create a playbook for every session we run. Use the link to find our playbook template to download. www.implement.dk/vf#design

TIME	POINT ON THE AGENDA	HOW	MATERIAL / TECH.
BEFORE			
DURING			
AFTER			

Figure 12.2   Our template for the playbook

Your playbook is a practical document where you have all the elements of the Design Star at the top of the page. Below you have columns, for the before, during and after phases of your session. In each of the sections, you add the point from the agenda, the timing for this, how you will run this aspect of the session and who is responsible for what and, finally, what materials and tech is needed to execute. In essence, it's a detailed plan of the session that breaks the agenda down into action points and practicalities (Figure 12.3).

The aim is that the playbook will give you a detailed plan to execute on the day. It is also a good tool if you are working as a team that will facilitate a session to ensure you're all aligned on what is going to happen, when, how and why.

The facilitator will create the playbook and be the primary person who uses it, but if there are co-facilitators, technical assistants, producers or other people who are involved in delivering the workshop or training session, you can share it with them too. Its main purpose is to give the facilitator a clear overview of the session before, during and after.

Creating your playbook

Follow the same structure as this book from Parts II–IV. Begin by thinking about what will happen before. That means how you'll prepare yourself and also how the participants should prepare. Are there any tasks they need to do in preparation? Think about how you'll be inviting everyone to your session and whether there is anything you would like to share with them physically. Also consider whether you need to do a dry run of your session. If you're using materials, will someone else create those or do you need to? What will they look like? How should you design your platforms? It's these kinds of practical considerations that you want to be thinking about initially.

TIME	POINT ON THE AGENDA	HOW	MATERIAL / TECH.
7 min	**Welcome**	1. Introduce the context 2. Ground rules 3. Introduce MS Teams and Menti 4. Say hello to your breakout team	Breakout
8 min	**Introducing the module**	1. What are your expectations for this module? 2. Learning objective 3. Agenda	Menti
15 min	**Part 1:** **Export setup and rationale**	1. The current export setup can be optimised and simplified 2. Export sales from affiliates give rise to compliance risks 3. Efficiencies and tax risks 4. Allows for three types of territories 5. Export setup (as of 1 July 2020) 6. Breakout: How does this affect me?	Breakout
10 min	**Part 2:** **Detailed new way of working and governance**	1. The following principles are in place 2. What does this mean for export hubs? 3. We have set controls up to monitor compliance 4. Quiz in the new change	Quiz
10 min	**Part 3:** **Customer visit policy**	1. A standard procedure should be followed when negotiating contracts with distributors 2. Additional guidelines are in place to ensure compliance	Chat
5 min	**Breakout**	1. Breakout: 'How would this change affect me?' 2. Plenary: Who would like to share an example of how this would affect you or share a comment about this?	Breakout rooms
5 min	**Quiz**	1. Quiz 2. Breakout: What questions do I have? 3. Plenary Q&A	Menti quiz Breakout
10 min	**Key takeaway**	1. Present the key takeaway 2. Evaluate your level of understanding of the three learning objectives	Chat Menti evaluate

Figure 12.3   Example of playbook

For the during phase, you'll be considering the process that you'll be using to run the session. Now is when you go into greater detail about how that process will work in practice. You'll need to consider the core process of the session and if you'll be using openers, energisers, closers etc. What questions will be asked during specific sections? How will the session flow in terms of time? What platform(s) will you be using during each time slot? For example, you might begin with the facilitator or an expert in a studio, and then go into breakout rooms. You need to know how long the participants will have in the breakout rooms, what sorts of questions they'll be working with and how you will follow up afterwards.

Again, the aim is that all of these elements are formulated and planned specifically so that you are ready on the day and have a solid plan to execute.

Finally the playbook includes 'after' – this involves considering what happens when the session has finished. This is when you should decide how you will follow up with your participants, evaluate the session and tell the participants what their input was used for at a later date. You can't end your playbook with the end of the session. It also needs to cover the effect and what will happen afterwards.

How-to guide: The playbook

1. Fill out each element of the virtual Design Star at the top of the document, so that you have the key design considerations gathered in the playbook prior to diving into the details.

2. Start by filling out the first column within the 'during' part of the playbook. This is like your typical agenda of

a meeting, with key topics and timings. If you already have this done in an agenda, or an invite you have had sent out in advance to the participants, then just paste it into the document.

3. When you have all the agenda items in place, you can start to design the sub-processes for each agenda item (the column headed 'How'), and who is responsible. For example, what processes should the participants go through as part of the 'Welcome'? (five-minute intro from the facilitator on the purpose, rules of engagement and programme, ½-minute from each of the participants on expectation or a chat-check-in, a conclusion by the facilitator before stepping to the actual programme). We often find that the best scripts are thought through down to the minute and this is even more important in a virtual setting. This frees up more mental capacity to be present in the actual session, as all the details have been considered. When doing the script, think about how each section from break to break has a motivation, a content, an engagement and a wrap-up part (these can be re-ordered).

4. Fill in the last column with 'Materials'. Think in terms of variety, not just PowerPoint, also other platforms, videos, physical elements you want to draw in etc. This is also your checklist of templates, platforms or instructions that you would like to have produced prior to the day.

5. The last step is to fill in the 'Before' and 'After' columns.

   a. Before: What should be sent out to the participants in preparation and what should you yourself prepare for the session; (set-up Mentimeter, plan the Miro board, make slides etc.), and agreements with key participants or stakeholders ahead of your session.

b. After: Even before your workshop, you should note down what is to happen immediately afterwards: Feedback, follow-up e-mail to participants, follow-up on key conclusions or deliverables from the session etc. Remember: The more complex your workshop, and the more participants there are, the more detailed your playbook needs to be.

Based on the playbook, you are now ready to prepare the materials and/or platforms that you'll need on the day.

If you have a good plan, this makes it easier for you to be on top during the session, as we'll discuss in Part III of this book. We're not saying you can't deviate from your plan if you need to, but having a plan with these accurate timings in it will make it much easier to do that while maintaining control of the session and ensuring it flows. The idea is to plan for as many considerations as possible, based on the Design Star.

How much time should you spend planning?

There is no set answer to this question. In our experience, it depends on the session. For instance, if it's a recurring meeting that you're having every week, your planning for the first in this series of meetings might take a while, as you need to create the plan and maybe create an online collaboration template, but the following week it will get quicker because you'll then have a template for an agenda that you can use in the form of your playbook. If it's a one-off workshop of high importance you might put considerable effort into making it right, and getting feedback on the design from peers before the session, to ensure you are hitting the purpose. If you are very experienced as a facilitator and familiar with the theme of the session you might need less detailed planning. If the opposite is the case it might take longer.

Generally, the more people who will be participating in a session, the longer you'll spend planning it. That's not only because you'll have more elements to consider, but because, as a facilitator, you're much more likely to be working as part of a team of people, and completing the Design Star and creating your playbook will involve collaboration back and forth; the need for a very specific plan increases if more people have a part to play.

For a regular meeting, with a few participants, the Design Star and playbook may not take you longer than an hour to complete. If you're planning a large-scale event for hundreds of people, however, you're more likely to spend days on planning this activity.

The more inexperienced you are as a facilitator, the longer we would recommend spending on the Design Star and playbook. At the beginning, we believe it's better to make it more detailed. Consider the follow-up questions you might ask and scenarios that might arise. Think about the level of prompts you will need to remind you what's coming next in your playbook. You might only need one or two words, or you might want a couple of sentences. Everyone is different, but we would suggest that when you're new to virtual facilitation you spend a little longer on this stage.

The importance of a clear playbook

When you are running workshops for hundreds of people, your playbook becomes an incredibly important document for aligning a large team. This is what tells everyone what is going to happen when. For large virtual events you cannot deviate from that plan unless you are forced to, because there are too many other people involved.

Do you always need a playbook?

If you're planning a meeting for a group of four or fewer participants, you may not need to complete an extensive playbook. The Design Star will give you a solid understanding of why you are having the meeting and it's important that you communicate this with the participants. In this instance, your playbook might be much looser. But we would always recommend that you have a plan to begin with, because then you have something to deviate from.

In a light version with no playbook, in addition to knowing the purpose of your session, we recommend preparing an extended agenda. For each item on the agenda, note whether it's an input point or a decision point and know what you want to achieve from each point. You should still allocate time to each item accordingly, even in smaller meetings. So while you might not have an exhaustive playbook, like you would for a large-scale event, you still have a timed plan for your meeting.

It's also important to remember that it's not necessarily the number of participants that dictates what level of planning you need to carry out. Even with only four of you, if the outcome is very important it is worth spending some extra time in the planning to make sure you achieve it.

Factor in time zones

One of the great things about virtual sessions is that you can include participants from all over the world in sessions, but this can add some complexity to the planning process. You need to consider the time zones of different participants and how you can structure your session to accommodate this.

For example, something simple like a lunch break suddenly becomes a little more complicated when you have some participants in Europe and others in Asia. We worked with a company recently that wanted to run a global executive session and they had a really great idea about serving local dishes to the participants and arranging for them all to receive the same dishes at the same point in the day. For instance, they were thinking of serving a Danish sausage to participants, until we pointed out that, based on their timings, that would mean the people in the US were being given it at about 7 a.m., while the ones in Taiwan would be receiving their food late in the evening. We suggested that they rethink the catering aspect of their event to account for these time differences. Maybe schedule in two longer breaks with time for food, and communicate this clearly beforehand.

13

Wrapping Up the Before Part

In Part II we have provided you with all our knowledge and experience on 'before'. We've discussed our approach to designing virtual sessions with engagement and impact. You might now know exactly why we state that planning takes time! The time you invest here will show as high-quality meetings with engagement and results.

Starting with the 'why', working your way through the virtual Design Star – alone or in collaboration with a team – will ensure a well-thought-through session. Using a playbook will help you get a specific and structured plan. This is not only a plan for the actual session – it starts before the session, covers the session itself and, finally, looks at what happens after the session. If your meeting or workshop is part of a series the 'before' and 'after' might collapse somewhat into 'between'. When you are done with the playbook you are ready to produce the invitation and the materials, and to make specific preparations such as designing the platform or exercises.

During the before phase it can be a huge advantage to get some feedback on the plan from some of the stakeholders – or even to have them in the loop talking about the session from a high-level perspective.

To help you get an overview we have collected our top take-aways from each chapter. These are things we think are especially important.

Chapter	Top takeaways / key questions
6: Designing Virtual Meetings and Workshops with Engagement and Effect	• Use the virtual Design Star as a framework to guide your design • Are you designing the session alone or in a team? • Can you get feedback from key stakeholders to agree on the design and plan? • Make sure you have time to design and plan!
7: Purpose	• What is the context for the workshop? • Why are we having this meeting? What is the impact of the meeting? • What do you hope the output will be for the workshop? • What will be the success criteria? Deliverables • What are the sub-purposes? • How do we prioritise different purposes?
8: Participants	• Who will attend? • How many? • How are they related to each other, both from a formal and social perspective? • How do they feel about the content / process of the workshop? • How are the tech skills and maturity levels?

Chapter	Top takeaways / key questions
9: Platform	• What mental platform should you create?
	• What platform is it possible to use in this organisation (IT rules, security, skillset, connection speed etc.)?
	• What functions / platform do you need?
	• Breakouts?
	• Whiteboard?
	• Poll?
	• Quiz?
	• Shared documents?
10: Process	• How do you want to involve the participants?
	• Selling? Telling? Testing? Consulting? Co-creation? Orientation? Training? Facilitation?
	• What are the corner flags?
	• What key process should you use?
	• What subprocess / micro-involvements should you use?
11: Partners	• What partners do you need?
	• Who plays what part?
	• What part should the important stakeholders play in the processes?
	• Who will be the lead facilitator?
	• Is there a content expert / co-facilitator / tech assistant?

(Continued)

Chapter	Top takeaways / key questions
12: Planning the Session	Create a playbook with a detailed script for your session. Create materials and design your platform / micro-involvement to support your purpose. Make it visual!

III

During – Running a Good Virtual Meeting

The during phase covers the day of your session, when you carry out your final preparations and facilitate your session. It's here that you, as the facilitator, ensure all your preparation and the use of people's time result in the desired effect. It's here that you meet your participants and it's here that you achieve your purpose. Now is the time to act, using your thorough planning to execute your session.

In this part of the book, we'll look at the elements you need to be aware of during the session in order to create energy and ensure you reach the purpose. Although we'll predominantly focus on the role of the facilitator, we'll also explain when others can get involved – stepping in as partners, such as co-facilitator, breakout facilitator, tech wizard and expert.

It's important to remember that even if you have support from a technical assistant or co-facilitator, it's still your responsibility as the lead facilitator to effectively manage the session to ensure you meet your goals and achieve what you set out to.

In this part of the book we'll talk you through each of the principles of our model: The Good Virtual Facilitator.

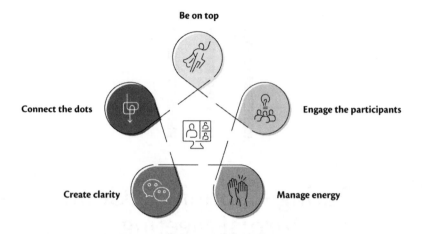

As the model illustrates the five principles are:

- **Be On Top**: On top of the process, the tech and the content.
- **Engage the Participants**: To reach your purpose through involvement, giving feedback, answering questions and creating variation.
- **Manage Energy**: Manage your own and your participants' energy to create an engaging session.
- **Create Clarity**: Guide your audience and make it easy to participate by giving clear instructions and making it clear where you are in the process, where you'll have discussions and make decisions, and who has what roles.
- **Connect the Dots**: Create meaning and flow through the session for your participants. Provide the context around the session to connect what's happened before to what will happen after.

14

Be On Top

Figure 14.1

To facilitate a good session, you as the facilitator need to be on top. 'Be on top of what?' you might be asking. There are many things you need to be on top of: the plan of the process, the tech, your participants, the content and the other elements that you bring to the session. When we talk about content in this context, we're not saying you need to be an expert in the content, but that you know the flow and what is happening.

When you are on top of all of this, you will have the capacity needed to run your session with a nice flow, and if something doesn't go quite according to your playbook, it's much easier to adjust.

Be on top of the process

Getting ready to go live

Everyone will do their final preparations for facilitating and running meetings slightly differently, but our advice would be to find some time on the morning of the session to read through your playbook and mentally run through what's going to happen during the session. It's also a good idea to check in with a potential co-facilitator or tech assistant, or your client if you're facilitating the meeting for someone else.

Even though you won't be going to a physical event, it's still important to allow plenty of time to set up your gear in the room from where you'll be hosting. Make sure that all the windows that you'll need for your session are open on your computer, not only the one you'll be running the session from, but also the ones that connect you to your team. Also check that the links you'll be using for your session (for shared PowerPoints, breakout rooms etc.) are working. We also recommend taking some time to prepare the space mentally too. Give yourself time to make sure that everything is set up, working and ready prior to the session.

Check that you have everything you need at hand before you start the meeting. You might have your playbook and speaking notes to one side and have your slides open and ready on your screen. Do whatever you need to feel both practically and emotionally ready to conduct the session.

We would recommend starting the meeting 15 minutes prior to the official start time, to give the other participants time to log in and have an informal chat. We also like to add some music here to create a nice atmosphere.

The reason it's so important to get yourself in a good mental state ahead of a session is because you bring your energy into the virtual space with you. If you're running late and feeling rushed, that energy will project into the session. It's well worth taking a little longer to get set up, maybe even being ready early. That way, you'll set yourself up for success from the beginning.

Be ahead as well as on top

As well as thinking about being 'on top', think about being 'ahead'. As the facilitator you not only need to be in the moment of the session, but you also need to be thinking ahead and be in the future. It's as though you're performing the dance and watching it from the balcony at the same time.

Questions to look ahead

- How are we doing on the flow?
- What do the participants need to know before the next phase?
- What is important for us to do or adjust now, for us to reach the purpose?
- Is it clear what we are talking about and how we should be working?
- Is everyone engaged and involved?
- How is the energy in the session?
- Who should I prompt to be ready for their 'part'?

Facilitating is about being in the moment, but you also need to have an awareness of the overall session. You need to constantly be considering whether you're moving the group in the right direction. You need to be thinking about what's coming up next to make sure your participants see and hear what they need to before moving on to the next stage.

It can be really difficult to do both at once. This is where small breaks for you as a facilitator come in handy. It can be while participants are working in breakout rooms or during the actual breaks. If you have a co-facilitator to run some of the elements during the session or to have this focus that's a huge advantage too.

This means from both a technical and a process perspective, you need to find that balance between being in the moment and having an idea of what's happening next and how that aligns with what's happening now. This is why your playbook is so useful, because it gives you that all-important overview of the session. You have to develop the art of being present and being able to zoom out at the same time when you're a good facilitator.

Revisit your playbook during the session

Having the playbook visible and available serves more than one purpose as a facilitator. It helps give you that overview that's so important to keep a session moving forward. But you shouldn't necessarily stick rigidly to the timings. You can check where you're supposed to be and decide whether the time you've allocated for a particular section of the meeting still makes sense. Maybe something requires more discussion than you anticipated, or maybe less. With your playbook, you're able to see how altering the timings will change the rest of your session.

You need to be in the moment to recognise that something needs more time, but then you also need to be on top to be able to look ahead and see where you could cut something else, or whether there is an item on the agenda that you can postpone. If you think about changing the agenda you can consider asking your participants if they're happy for agenda item five, for example, to be postponed to a future session to give you more time to spend on agenda item four, or they would rather cut item four off now and move on. This way you are creating a shared ownership to the process instead of you just making the decision. Whether you involve your participants depends on the context and timeline of the project, but it is always recommended to inform them about changes in the agenda.

> *Top tip: If, on the day of a session of any size, something completely unexpected happens, don't panic. The best way to handle this kind of scenario is to take a five-minute break and make a new plan that supports where you are now and that will still allow you to deliver the purpose of your session.*

If you do change the plan, really focus on the timings. Keeping track of time is one of the aspects that people struggle most with when it comes to facilitation. If you are late back from a break, or one part of your session has run over, make sure you update the times in your playbook and work out how it will change from there.

Do you need a second facilitator?

When you're working with another facilitator, whether they're providing support with the tech or co-facilitating the session, it's important that you're in regular communication with one another. In terms of the tech, that might mean asking if the next exercise is ready. Or you might check in to find out if you're running on time. If you're co-facilitating, it's important to flag any important feedback that might appear in the chat to the main facilitator in case they don't see it immediately. This kind of feedback can also really help the facilitator get a sense of the mood in the room and alter their approach accordingly.

What if you can't have a co-facilitator?

If it's not possible for you to have a co-facilitator or support with your tech, a good tip is to introduce a few more breaks. When you have short breaks at appropriate points throughout your session, it can allow you to calibrate, adjust your playbook and look at what is coming up in order to decide whether you need to make changes to the agenda. Giving yourself short spaces of breathing time can really help if you don't have someone else to support you with the facilitation. Or you could use breakout sessions to give you a bit of time while the participants engage in an activity among themselves.

Be on top of tech

Being on top of tech is an essential part of your role as the facilitator. By now you should feel 100% comfortable using your tech. Just do a final check that the videos, links etc. you'll use in the session are working. You should feel as though you can deviate from your plan and improvise, and to do that you need to know your options in relation to your tech. A dry run can help you check if it works. Knowing the typical problems with using your platform can also help you to guide your participants if they have any difficulties.

As well as making sure you are on top of tech, it's time to see whether your participants can use the links, log on and access the platform wherever they're working from. Even if you send clear instructions prior to your session, your participants may still have issues. There's nothing worse than being at the start of your session and realising that you're missing half of your participants because they're not able to log on. That's so stressful and doesn't get your session off to the best start. Think about what you might need to problem solve with your participants too. If they're having trouble logging in, what can you suggest that they try?

Our advice is to encourage your participants to trouble-shoot using the chat – via personal messages if possible. Kicking off a session with participants complaining about tech issues in plenary is not a good way to set the energy for the session, so do what you can to avoid this.

> *Top tip: Send the link (and password if needed) in the Outlook invite for the meeting, so that your participants don't have to search through dozens of emails to find what they need.*

Don't be afraid to get the other participants to chip in here too. Often when people are having tech issues they will post a comment in the chat, and other participants can reply to them.

There might be times when you need to be more on top of this than others. If your participants are all new to a tech platform, the chances that you'll need to troubleshoot and assist some of them are greater than if you're using a platform that you're all familiar with and have used extensively before. In this case we recommend that a part of the session is a tour of the platform at the beginning of the session to ensure everyone knows how to adjust the slides and video for the best possible visuals and the key features to use.

Being on top of your tech really is vital though, because tech issues can be incredibly derailing for a session. Remember that without your participants you don't have a session, so knowing your tech is essential.

If you're new to virtual facilitating, and you're new to a platform, don't be afraid to tell the participants that. Just say something along the lines of, 'Okay people, I'm new at this so just give me a moment to handle the tech side.' By verbalising this, you remove some of the pressure from yourself and show the participants you are working on it and are on top of things, even though it might take you a few moments longer to get the tech right.

Virtual facilitation isn't about running flawless and perfectly produced sessions. It's about owning the meeting and taking responsibility for it. Sometimes taking responsibility means acknowledging that you just need a moment to sort technical issues.

Case study: Troubleshooting

We were running a session for what we thought would be 60 participants, but we actually ended up with 70 participants because 10 of them had chosen to be in the same room using one computer. The instructions in the invitation explicitly stated that everyone should be on their own device, but this part was not read or accepted by all participants. In the session, we had to deal with it. A key element of this session was personal breakout discussions, so using the chat we divided the group of ten into two groups of five and told them to have their discussions in smaller groups. Although it wasn't ideal, we figured it out and made the session work.

Be on top of content

As a pure facilitator, you don't necessarily need to know much of the content. In fact, sometimes it can be better to know less, because this prevents you from forming an opinion. A pure facilitator will only ask questions and drive the process. But the more you move towards being a trainer or an expert, the more you tend to know the content and the harder it is to remain in that pure facilitator role.

The key to facilitating a good virtual meeting when it comes to the content is knowing what you need to be on top of and who owns it. You need a solid understanding of your role and the level to which you need to be involved, which are all things you should have worked out when you were completing your Design Star and playbook.

> *Top tip: Be clear and tell your participants what role you are playing 'now'.*

If there is someone else delivering a presentation or owning the content, as the facilitator ensure that you have set the right ground rules to allow you to steer them back on track. That means you will have discussed beforehand how much time will be dedicated to each part of the meeting, as well as how you will keep everything on track. You might agree with the speaker that you can gently intervene to bring them back on topic, for instance. This all comes back to the different partners you have in your session and making sure that you are all aligned with the playbook.

For example, if you have all agreed that one person should talk for 20 minutes, then as the facilitator you can help them to stay on track and give them gentle prompts or nudges to indicate how long they have left.

How to be on top of time

There are also tools that you can use to help keep your session on track, such as timers or a technique called timeboxing. For example, you could say, 'You've all got 20 minutes now to go on your breakout and do this.' Make sure that you tell your participants how long they have to share their thoughts, three minutes per person for example, and also tell them that you'll let them know when their three minutes is up. Finally, in breakout rooms it can be effective to ask groups to name a timekeeper – great conversations can be difficult to stop if no one is in charge.

Another way to keep track of time is using interventions. If you frame it right it can be effective without becoming disengaging. For example, you could say something like, 'I'll just stop you there for a moment because I'm not sure how this relates to this agenda item. Can you help me understand or can we put it in the parking lot for now?' That's a gentle way of cutting in and steering the discussion back on track, without dismissing what someone is saying.

You can even start with your framing from the beginning of the meeting, by highlighting that you will only have an opportunity to look at the problems during this session, or that you are only going to focus on the positive side of an idea. Or even that there are no limitations for a particular topic. If you have framed the content, it will help you to stay on top of it and keep the session moving in the right direction.

Suggestions for how to be on top of time

- Timebox activities using a timer
- Make participants responsible for keeping time
- Say 'We only have time for three more people to share their opinion. . .'
- Say 'Sorry to interrupt you, X, but in the interests of time, we need to close the discussion and move to the next agenda item. Is that ok?'
- Indicate with your hand – in clear view of your webcam – holding up two fingers to indicate there are two minutes left.
- Frame your session clearly to let participants know the purpose – remind them if needed 'Today we are only looking at the problems. Next time we'll focus on the solutions.'

Suggestions for how to be aware of time

15

Engage the Participants

Figure 15.1

Engagement is crucial to get people to follow you, give you the input and reach the result. If you believe that business is about people, then you know that business is about engagement. Without engagement, few things will change. We believe that it's key to the process of facilitation and that it's your responsibility as the facilitator to make engagement happen.

What we hear from our clients is that they find it difficult to create engagement during virtual sessions. Partly due to the fact that people expect very effective sessions and partly due to the fact that they don't know how to do it. We believe it is crucial for a good virtual session to engage the participants and find those workarounds that can make it happen in a virtual setting. And yes, you can also do an energiser in a virtual meeting.

There are several elements that you need to be aware of when it comes to engaging the participants in your session and holding that engagement.

Know the attention span

In a virtual meeting our attention span – how long we can focus and concentrate for – is very limited. Usually, in a physical setting, the rule of thumb is that adults can concentrate for around 20 minutes. In a virtual setting that average is even lower, because it's much harder to concentrate and remain engaged when you're not physically involved and socially connected. Figure 15.2 illustrates how our attention span drops during virtual meetings.

What you can see from this graph is that people's attention is rising at the start of a virtual meeting, but after just five minutes it will start to drop and it will lower to a point where, if you don't engage the participant, they will almost flatline after 20 minutes. This means that if you do a 45-minute talk backed with PowerPoint slides the attention of the participants will be low during most of the session. This happens even if the theme

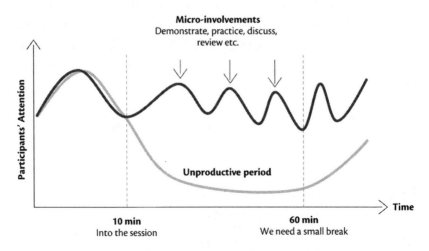

Figure 15.2   The attention span during virtual sessions

is interesting – the brain simply doesn't like to pay attention passively for this long.

Luckily, as a facilitator, you can do something to avoid people becoming unproductive. The key word here is variation. Providing variation throughout your session will keep people engaged. As the graph illustrates you can create a small break to gain some attention. Yet the best way to keep participants' attention throughout your session is to use micro-involvements, often throughout the entire session.

We suggest leaving around five to ten minutes between each micro-involvement. This might sound quite frequent, but each of these does not have to take long. One minute can be enough. Sometimes it can be as simple as asking 'What questions do you have right now?' or 'What are your thoughts around this?' or you could break up the session with a question in the chat, an energiser or by conducting a poll. Introducing longer process methods during the session where participants work by themselves in breakout rooms or on shared documents is also an effective way to increase their attention span. When participants are active themselves, they can stay attentive much longer than 5–10 minutes, so here you can give people time to work for 20–30 minutes or so.

What we suggest is to be aware of how long people can be present and engaged and that you find ways of engaging them in the session. Simply saying something like, 'I just have ten slides to go through and then we're finished, can you hold on?' isn't enough to engage people in a virtual meeting. All you're doing there is showing people something that they can't absorb.

Top tip: Use variation in your session. You can touch people emotionally, physically and intellectually and each of these will help to engage your participants. You might get them to physically move their bodies or you might be giving people an opportunity to express themselves and talk to someone.

Make your session relevant

Relevancy is just as important as variation in a virtual session. The acronym to remember for relevancy is WIIFM – What's In It For Me?

Very early in your session, you need to address why people are there, what they can bring to the table and why they should listen. This is about making it relevant but it's also about motivation. Consider how you can explain the relevancy to your participants in a way that they can relate to. Give them opportunities to relate to it, time to reflect, or even time to answer for themselves why they should be listening and paying attention.

Hopefully your participants already have an idea why they are in your session based on your invitation and pre-work, but it's important to reiterate that during the session.

> *Top tip: A good way to ensure WIIFM is to start your session by stating the overall purpose, but not just in a broad sense, in a specific sense so that every single person knows their specific purpose within the session too.*

As we talked about in Chapter 8, you will often begin your meeting with an opener. It's common in virtual meetings for people to have back-to-back meetings in a day, which means when they arrive in your session their mind could be somewhere completely else. Use an opener to get people into the session and set their mindset for what's ahead. Use questions like 'Why is this topic important to you?' that will get them ready to participate in the session.

The importance of effective questions

As the facilitator, one of the best (and quickest) ways of engaging participants is to ask effective questions. Asking good questions is an important skill that needs to be nurtured and trained. We have all experienced the dead silence in a room, physical or virtual, when the facilitator asks, 'Any questions?' Yet with a little more skilled questioning technique you can gain valuable inputs from your participants. It's about both the questions asked and the process you create around it.

Guide to good questions

Here are some tips for creating good questions:

- Ask open questions. Your questions should never be closed. Asking something like 'Do you think this is a good idea?' is a bad question because it's closed and people only have to answer with 'Yes' or 'No'. You want your question to lead to interaction. Make sure you frame it so that people have to give a full answer.
- Direct your questions to the area you want to talk about. Ask, 'What do you think could work with this idea?' or 'What opportunities can you see in this idea?' As the facilitator you need to be very aware of what you're looking for and what sort of discussions you want to encourage.
- Think carefully about how you frame your questions. We sometimes see people taking engagement out of their sessions because they don't feel that they can control the direction of the meeting if they ask these kinds of open questions. This is why it's so important to think about how you frame your question to direct the discussion. A few other examples could include, 'What three benefits do you see coming out of this situation?' or 'What key learnings do you take away from this?' or 'What actions are you taking away from this?' or 'What was the most important topic in your discussion right now?'. These questions prompt a reply whereas questions like 'Anyone want to share?' prompt a 'NO' in the mind and create awkward silence.

Top tip: Prepare your key questions for your session and write them down in your playbook and speaker notes.

This level of direction in the discussions is less scary than having a totally open forum where someone has started by asking, 'Any questions?' and it makes it easier for you to reach the purpose of the session.

Have a process for asking good questions

By making sure your participants know what questions you'll be talking about, you'll help them feel safe to participate in a discussion with the rest of the group. It's really hard to read a virtual room and that can make participants worry that they will be the only person with a particular question or comment.

How you ask the question is just as important as the question itself. It's important to have a framework in place to start generating engagement in a virtual room.

Top tip: Put your question on a slide to make it clear to all the participants what you're asking.

As well as having a clear question, you need a process that facilitates engagement from your participants. The key here is that you take charge of the situation and consider giving your participants time to reflect on it. You might start by sharing your own thoughts just briefly, or you could give them 30 seconds in silence, or you could put them in breakout rooms where they can discuss the question with just one or two other people before coming back into the main session. Using breakout rooms can be a good way for people to get reassurance that their thoughts are ok. Saying something out loud is easier in a smaller group and can give them the confidence to share their thoughts with a bigger group. Breakout rooms allow people to think out loud without doing so in a completely public setting. Coming back from the breakout discussion you would normally have more courage to share since you have validated your thoughts or might even phrase it with a 'we' instead of an 'I'. All these examples show that the facilitator needs to create clarity and trust around the form and the topic.

Engage your audience with the use of questions

1. Make sure you let the participants know when in the agenda you will open up for questions, and tell them how to do it. (Raise hand/Write in the chat/Just unmute themselves.)

2. Framing. Ask clear questions / give clear instructions. What do you want people to talk about? What area should the questions be within? Is everything up for questioning?

3. Give time for people to think individually or consider allowing people into breakout rooms to discuss any questions first, and then opening it up in plenary. It can create safety to talk about the questions in smaller groups before they share their perspectives with everyone.

4. Open up. 'We've got time for a few questions. Three more. . .' You control who should unmute and speak.

5. Answers. If we want to provide an answer here and now, you have the following options:

   a. You answer it yourself = Is a fast way of going through Q&A

   b. Give it over to someone who has more knowledge about it = Creates credibility that you don't believe you know everything and recognise the experience in the group

   c. Ask the crowd or create a poll = Is an opportunity to engagement everyone

   d. Encourage the participants to find the answer themselves by using guiding questions = Self-discovery

---

Tell people when they can ask questions

In our meetings, we typically have a very tight and planned agenda. If a participant clicks the 'raise hand' button or does it physically on the video to ask a question, how do you deal with that? Our approach is to make sure that all the participants know at what point in the agenda they are able to ask questions. At the start, explain that throughout the session you'll have slots for Q&A, or tell them that it's ok for them to raise their hand if they have a question at any point. You need to tell them how they should engage and how they should question, as well as being clear about the direction of their questions. Sometimes you might also consider answering a question with another question – 'would it be all right if I got back to you on this after I'm done with this topic?', 'Could we take this just the two of us after?', 'Should we take some questions now and dive into them with the risk of us not having time for the last point on the agenda?'. All these questions have the intent to share and create buy-in to the solution, which oftentimes is relevant.

How to encourage your participants to open up

We recommend using breakout rooms to get participants to open up, as smaller groups often make people feel safer, as we explained in Chapter 10. It's a good place to engage participants as there are fewer of them, it gives room for open discussion and creates inputs for questions as people get a chance to test their ideas in a smaller group.

There are a few things you can do to manage breakout rooms during your session:

Be really clear on your instructions and make sure they are visual – preferably also in the breakout room.

Before you send them out, you should use the function inside the meeting software conference call that enables some kind of timer, or ask people to set a timer on their phones for five minutes, for instance, and to return to the main meeting room when their alarm goes off. Give people clear instructions and tell people how they can get help if they need it.

Once people are in their breakout rooms, go visit to check if they are working on the right task and also give them a heads-up two minutes before the end of the exercise. Tell them how much time they have left. It's your job as the facilitator to go out and check in with the groups. This is a chance to see whether there are any questions or misconceptions, especially at the start. It's important to follow up with your participants and listen to them when they go into breakouts. This is a unique opportunity to listen and see what's happening, but don't just be a ghost. Make sure you tell them before that you'll be coming around, say hi when you arrive, listen in and help out if they have any questions.

When you are back in plenary after a breakout session and you have been using text for inputs, such as the chat or a shared document or tool for providing text inputs, like Menti, it can be nice to refer to what people have written here. For instance, you could say, 'I saw that somebody wrote X, Y, Z. Who was that and could you elaborate please?' It's another way to steer the focus and direction of the conversations in your session.

How to deal with ad-hoc questions

Sometimes you might have questions coming in during your session and think that these are answers you should provide to the whole group. If you want to answer a question, as the facilitator you have a few options. The first is to just answer the question yourself, which is a fast way of addressing these types of questions. If you're in a breakout room, consider if the question might be relevant to recap in plenary.

But there are other options and sometimes these can be more suitable. One option is to pass the question over to someone who has more knowledge about it. This can actually add to your credibility if you say, 'I don't have all the answers here, but so-and-so does.'

Another option, which isn't one that you would have in a physical setting, is to have a quick poll. This allows you to engage with the whole group and to see if the question is actually relevant to talk about in the session. If you have the opportunity and are a little bit tech savvy, we strongly encourage you to use polls like these throughout the session. You could introduce them by saying something like, 'Let's just quickly see what the group thinks of that question' or 'Please vote on a scale of 1–5 how often you meet this challenge.'

It is worth pointing out that polls like these are anonymous and if you are going to have anonymous inputs then you need to be very aware of the questions you're posing. You need to be prepared for the fact that people might be more critical, because it's easier to be critical when you are anonymous. Always think about the sort of space or room that you're opening up.

The final option is to answer a question with a question. You might use this if you don't have the answer yourself and want to encourage participants to find the answer for themselves. You can encourage self discovery by asking questions such as, 'Why are you posing that question?' or 'Why do you feel that's important?' Don't be afraid of saying that you don't have the answer and you'll need to come back to them later, if that's what you need to do.

How to engage your participants in exercises during the session

Exercises are important for keeping your participants engaged, as we discussed in Chapter 10.

The aim of using exercises can be to produce something or get participants into a specific mindset. In the before phase you already planned the exercises – now you're going to use them. This is about how you execute that plan and guide people through the exercises, making sure that the energy and involvement remains high and that it all flows nicely. Introducing an exercise is the first step and this is a quite important one. This is where you make it important to participants (or not) by answering why this exact activity is relevant. Tell people *why* they should engage in this exercise and *why* you find it important. If you want people to be engaged, telling them why is a good place to start. Stating that 'next we are to do an exercise' is not enough.

Next step is to explain what the process of the exercise will look like. We are looking more at this in Chapter 17 on creating clarity, so here we just want to state that engagement also includes knowing what is expected – what to do. Finally, you let people off to start working themselves. This is often where you gain a lot of engagement if you succeeded with explaining the why and the process. We often say that 'this is where the magic happens'.

One thing that's key to your success as a facilitator by getting engagement from your audience, is whether you believe in the process/exercise yourself. If you don't do that, you will probably not come across as credible and you won't get people to follow you. If you do believe in it people will feel this and follow you.

Often it can help to convey the purpose in doing a specific exercise across to the participants and show that you know it's going to work. When you do this, you can get people to do almost anything. However, if people get the sense that you're just going through the motions but don't truly believe in something, then they resist.

We often hear people say that something like 'this idea might work with employees but it won't work with our group of CEOs'. By experience we disagree. We are all humans, regardless of our job titles. If you believe in what you're doing as the facilitator, it will work just as well for the CEOs as it will for the employees or the middle managers.

Sometimes even if you've prepared well and done your due diligence with choosing the right type of exercise, things might not go to plan. You might find some of the participants are shy or hesitant. This is why it's important to check in with your participants once you have set up an exercise. Give them feedback and check that the instructions are clear, that everything makes sense and that they are ready to go. You can have this kind of feedback either in the chat or in front of the webcam, so they can give non-verbal feedback on whether they are ready to go.

Using micro-involvements

Micro-involvements are an easy and effective way to engage participants That might be via polls, quizzes, chat, whiteboards, breakouts or individual reflections. Whatever micro-involvements you use, make sure they match your process.

If you are comfortable using them, you can improvise throughout the session, introducing everything from individual reflection or a quick poll to breakouts if they are appropriate. But you shouldn't just use these because you think they're fun or different. You need to make sure that every micro-involvement supports the purpose of the agenda and is explained with a *why*.

You'll find lots of information on micro-involvements and the other exercises and energisers you can introduce to your sessions in our online resources. www.implement.dk/vf#methods

16

Manage the Energy

Figure 16.1

Now you know about being on top and creating engagement. The next step is to focus on the energy. This is somewhat connected to engagement, but deserves its own chapter as it is crucial for a good session. As the facilitator, energy is an important parameter to keep in mind and be able to work with in different ways to suit yourself and your audience. Remember that energy is something that you can influence. You have the ability to turn it up, turn it down and direct it towards the important stuff during your session. Just as with engagement, variation is key.

Too much or too little energy in a meeting can be counterproductive. As the facilitator, you need to make sure that the energy level is just right for the activities you've designed. Do you need creative energy for ideas on implementation of a new strategy? Do you need deep focus for difficult problem-solving? Both these scenarios call for different energy, and as the facilitator it's your job to create the right energy during the session.

This aspect of virtual facilitation is very much about sensing your audience and working with energy. Energy is relatively closely connected to involvement and engagement, but it's subtly different. When we talk about energy we often talk about it on four levels:[1]

- Physical energy: How much energy do we have?
- Emotional energy: Are we connected with ourselves and with others?
- Mental energy: How much focus do we have on what we're doing? Are we multitasking or working deeply and focusing?
- Purpose energy: Does what we're doing make sense?

Working with energy in a session is a really nice way to support engagement and involvement. If you have the right level of energy in your sessions, you'll also find that they run more smoothly and that it's easier to reach a common goal. There are several things you can do to be aware of the energy and to support the energy of yourself and the other participants.

Reframe your mindset about what energy feels like

If you are used to running physical sessions, you may need to reframe your mindset around energy for virtual sessions. In a physical room you will often feel the energy very evidently whereas this is less so in a virtual session. Don't take silence as a

---

[1] *The Power of Full Engagement: Managing Energy, Not Time, Is the Key to High Performance and Personal Renewal*, James E. Loehr and Tony Schwartz, Simon and Schuster, 2005.

bad sign, for example. In a virtual session it is often the case that no news is good news. Silence can mean that your participants are engaged in the virtual world.

You also have to accept that you won't get the same boost of energy from your participants that you do in physical sessions. For instance, when you start group discussions in the physical session you hear people's voices rising as they have discussions, and you feel that energy comes back to you. You don't get this in a virtual setting, and we know from experience that it takes some time to accept that this does not mean that nothing is happening.

You can't compare your experiences of facilitating physical sessions with virtual sessions. We often hear facilitators telling us that they are bad in a virtual setting and that they can't feel the energy. This is especially the case in plenary meetings, where there often isn't much obvious engagement from participants. But if you look at what happens in the chat or breakouts, you'll see that this is where a lot of the magic and the engagement happens. You need to set your expectations differently and postpone your judgment of the meeting. In a physical meeting, you're constantly judging how it's going, but in the virtual you need to postpone that judgment until you have had the chance to get feedback from the participants afterwards.

Top tip: When you're delivering a virtual session, you are often alone in a room. It can be hard to feel the same emotional state, as if you have 50 participants in front of you and it can feel very monotone. To help create the right level of energy, imagine how you would feel if you were physically standing in front of an audience of that size. Try to tap into the emotion and feeling within yourself.

How to sense the energy in a session

In a physical meeting, it seems easier to sense the energy of your session. But in a virtual space many people report that they have a hard time 'feeling' their participants. The simple solution to this is to ask your participants how they are feeling throughout the session:

- What is your energy level right now on a scale of one to five?
- Are we focusing on the most important topics?
- Do you need a break, yes or no?

You could use the chat or micro-involvements to get feedback from the participants quickly. You can also listen into breakout rooms and ask people for feedback. Don't just ask these questions in plenary and expect everyone to open up though.

Another simple step is to make sure everyone has their video cameras on, so you can see people. This is very important for helping you sense energy levels and helping you get some signs from the participants in the session about how they are feeling and engaging, otherwise it can feel rather cold and like you're just giving but not getting anything back.

When you're delivering a session for a larger group, it can be more challenging to check in on their energy levels. It's not quite so easy to ask how everyone is feeling verbally when you have over 100 people online, for instance. In these cases, polls are a really useful tool. Ask people to rate their energy levels on a scale of one to five. Another option is to ask them if they'd like a break now, mark with yes or no.

Adjust the energy to match the session

Knowing that the energy can feel low for the facilitator if you compare it to a physical session, it's important that you don't go into a session and mirror the energy of your participants. Your job is to bring them to the state you need for the session.

Sometimes you might need higher energy to get people started and get them involved. Other times you might find that everyone starts with good energy levels. Often this is connected to how important your meeting is to them. If they feel that the content is important, they might have good energy and be really looking forward to your meeting. By contrast, if this is a session that they've been told they have to attend and they didn't have a choice about it, their energy might be very different.

Our advice is that, as the facilitator, your personal energy should demonstrate 20% above of what you expect from the participants. You need to own the energy in the virtual room and you need to adjust it to the different roles you play whether it is opening the session, providing expert advice or giving instructions. Every role requires a different energy.

Don't try to make your energy too much higher than theirs, otherwise it can come across as not being authentic or being inappropriate. Remember that the participants will be looking at you a lot of the time and they can be lifted up by how you come across smiling, looking into the camera and talking directly to them.

We recommend using your personality and presence to bring your participants along with you, whether you're trying to create a higher level of energy in the session, create room for reflection or create a space for openness. Our advice is to role model the energy that you'd like to have.

Creating the right energy from the start

There is a lot you can do as the facilitator, from the very beginning of your session, to create the right energy as your participants enter the virtual space.

If you are running a physical meeting, you would always welcome people as they come into the room, give them a handshake and make them feel welcome. It's no different in the virtual meeting. Think about the virtual equivalent of that handshake and it's simple: just say hi, welcome and thanks for joining. When you join a virtual room where there's a little bit of talk going on, it doesn't feel awkward and that paves the way for a high-quality meeting. You might even say that the meeting starts before it officially starts.

> *Top tip: Place a Post-it note with a smile besides the webcam, or a picture of one or more of the participants on the wall or even a real person behind the camera to remind you to smile and visualise the audience.*

If you're waiting for people to join, simply saying, 'We'll just give it a couple of minutes' shows your participants that you're on top of things and that you're taking responsibility for starting on time and succeeding with what you set out to do.

At the start of the session you also want to focus on the emotional energy, and making your participants feel safe to participate in the session. It's good to show them that they're in the right session, so have a PowerPoint slide with the title of the session on your screen, and maybe even a picture of the host if they aren't there yet. Or you could include a visual representation of what you're going to talk about. That might be a nice image on your slide or even a video. This just helps people to feel welcome. You can also use music to trigger positive emotions.

> *Top tip: Say welcome to people as they join, smile and maybe even put a message in the chat so that they know they can engage on there as well.*

Once everyone is present, ask them to present themselves at the beginning of the session and say where they're calling in from. This helps people to start relating to one another.

Using music in sessions

Music is not only relevant at the beginning of a session. You can use it at other points in your session to create an emotion or to direct focus. If we're asking people to do individual reflections, we would put some music on in the background. Sometimes we might put upbeat music on during the break as well.

There are three main reasons why we use music in our sessions:

1. To facilitate a state or emotion. Use music to support your participants in reaching a happy/focused/relaxed state at different points in the session.
2. To cue up what is about to happen. That might mean that when they hear music, it's a sign they have two minutes to finish what they're doing, or that when the music is playing they need to work.
3. To increase focus and learning. Use music to tune out all the other noises and help the participants to completely focus on what's about to happen.

Some examples of situations when you might use music

- Entry into the meeting
- Transitions
- Individual reflections/work
- Breaks
- Energisers
- Endings

Factors to consider when choosing music

We suggest that the music you're choosing will support what you're talking about or doing. Also think about whether it should have lyrics or be instrumental, as well as what the tempo or pace of the music is. Does this fit with the energy and atmosphere you're trying to create?

Finally, consider whether your participants will be familiar with the music you're choosing, especially if it's lyrical. Sometimes it can be good for people to sing along and other times it creates a distraction. These are all things to consider when you're selecting music for use at different points in your session.

We have put together some example playlists online to give you an indication of the kind of music that you could use. www.implement.dk/vf#methods

Think about your appearance

When it comes to creating the right energy, your own appearance on screen matters as well. In a virtual setting, we are stripped of some of our body language, which means that your appearance and what you have left becomes even more important.

Think about how you dress, how you look and what's behind you in order to come across with the energy that you're aiming to role model for the session.

You can still use body language in a virtual session; you just need to make sure you position yourself correctly. If you're very close to your camera, then the participants won't be able to see much more than your face and neck; if you move further away they can see more of your body and that allows you to use hands and body language to a greater degree.

> *Top tip: Place yourself so people can see your hands – and use them to articulate. This creates a completely different impression than if you 'just' see a face talking.*

As we mentioned in Part I, you have the option of putting your computer on a box to raise it up and that means you have the luxury of being able to stand up to deliver your session. Just standing up will automatically introduce some more energy into the session. Also, if you want to be able to move around more using a flip or changing the distance to the camera to create variation, get a mic that's not connected to your computer with a wire. This will give you the freedom to move around the room and use your body language during the session.

Be strategic, yet authentic

Normally you would say that authenticity is a good thing and something to strive for, but when you're a facilitator you might want to create a special energy in the room or a special focus. It's your job to make sure that your energy matches the energy that you want to create. For instance, if you are high energy and tend to talk loudly and use active body language, there might be situations where you need to tone it down.

There's a balance to strike here. You still want to smile and relax so that you don't come across as inauthentic, but you also shouldn't just go into these sessions with the attitude of 'this is me, I can't help it'. You need to adjust your energy and behaviour to take the session where it needs to go. You need to be strategic, manage your tone and your energy, and use yourself to make sure the right energy comes across in the session.

Use humour to own the energy

Humour is a big part of owning the energy in a session as a facilitator. Smiling and humour are the fastest ways to connect with people, and they are great tools for creating some looser energy and opening up a virtual space. If you tell a funny story about yourself, it can be a good way to make the session feel a little less formal. It breaks the ice and helps everyone to open up a little more. However, think carefully about the kind of humour you use. It can be easily misunderstood when a lot of the signals you'd have in the physical world are missing in the virtual space.

When you're potentially connecting with people from all over the world, bear in mind that the cultural differences in humour can be quite sizable. Sarcasm and irony can often be difficult for people to pick up on, so it's important to do something humorous relating to your own situation, rather than focusing on someone else in the session or introducing humour that falls between the lines.

Five simple tips to come across with more energy

- Stand up and use your body language actively.
- Speak in a higher pitch and at a faster pace.
- Visualise the feeling you would normally have in front of an audience of this size.
- Be informal and use humour relating to your own situation.
- Smile.

Top tip: Don't try to guess how people are feeling. Just ask them.

The importance of breaks

Breaks are a time for people to recharge energy, both their mental capacity and their physical needs, such as going to the bathroom, moving their body, getting water, coffee or even a snack. We're sure you've all been in sessions where the facilitator says, 'People, should we just skip the break and keep going?' Although skipping breaks might seem like an easy way to gain time, it's not a good idea and it will just lead to a slump in energy and engagement among your participants. This is why you should never skip the break in your session.

We recommend the following.

- Have a break every 45 minutes to an hour during a virtual session.
- Keep breaks short – seven minutes is sufficient.
- Use a countdown timer to keep on top of the break time.
- Plan more frequent, shorter breaks.

There are two main reasons for having more frequent but shorter breaks. One is that it encourages people to physically move, and the other is that being in virtual meetings can be quite intensive as they are usually delivered at a fast pace and there is a lot going on.

In a physical session, it's much easier for people to stand up, move around and swap seats if they're having conversations. In the virtual world, you're not going to move to another part of the room when you join a breakout, so encourage people to be physically active during their breaks.

> *Top tip: Suggest that in the short seven-minute break participants get up, stretch their legs, make a cup of coffee, walk around and then come back. Use the breaks as a way of creating that physical state change for them.*

Using energisers

The longer your session, the more important it is that you put these energisers in there. These activities are a quick way to create trust and engagement between the participants in a session. Even though they might seem fun and without purpose, there is a purpose behind them. It's really important to create positive emotions among the participants in general – physical activity increases brain activity and this will help the rest of the meeting to move swiftly forward.

Respect the context and your audience when you're deciding which energisers to do. It's important to read your audience and build from there. In many cases this will be the first time that your participants have tried a virtual energiser. Start with something that is not too threatening or extreme and build from there.

> *Top tip: Have a list of small energisers to use during the session when you feel like people need some energy.*

Make sure you frame your energisers and explain why you're doing them. Tell people that you're doing this to get everyone focused for the next part, or to help everyone get to know one another a little better. When you frame it in the right way, people really enjoy these energisers, even if you get them doing some rather strange things. Be a role model and go first if you're asking people to do something. It's important that you step up and commit yourself.

We often have people telling us that the participants in our sessions won't want to do these exercises. Yet we have yet to experience this – actually they all participate and, what's more, they all enjoy them and remember the session as a result. Be brave and plan these energisers into your sessions.

Don't be afraid to mix different types of energisers too, such as the competitions with the physical. Be creative! You can read more about energisers in Chapter 10 and find specific suggestions of energisers in our online resources. www.implement.dk/vf#methods

17

Create Clarity

Figure 17.1

Creating clarity during your session is important to ensure your participants know where you are at each stage of the process, how you expect them to contribute, and that they are clear on what's been decided or achieved so far.

In a virtual space, we lack all the non-verbal signals that we send to each other when we are physically together. The small nod – that we understand and are ready to proceed – is gone, just as is the confused look on people's faces right after you pose a question that is too long or just difficult to understand. Because we don't have these non-verbal signals to rely on, and people tend to talk less, it's even more important that you, as the facilitator, guide your participants through the session with clear instructions and make it easy for them to contribute.

The main reason you need to be clear in every aspect of your session is to ensure you have your participants' full attention. As soon as people can't see how one thing connects to another, what is expected from them or how you're taking a decision, their mental capacity shrinks and they disengage.

Being clear around decision-making is particularly important. If people have come into a meeting believing that they are going to make a decision on something, only to discover part-way through that they're not, then they aren't likely to want to participate. This doesn't create a good platform for continuing people's involvement with a project. If participants leave a session and they aren't clear on the decisions that have been taken, then they may also not follow them, because they aren't aware of them. This is why you, as the facilitator, have to be aware that a lack of clarity here can result in other complications following a session.

Create a shared idea of how you will work together

Creating clarity isn't only about providing clear instructions, it's also about creating a clear shared idea of how you will all work together during this particular meeting. As a facilitator there are actions that you can take that are proactive and actions that you can take that are reactive.

We would always recommend taking a proactive approach as far as possible. The first step here could be to use ground rules to set your expectations about how participants should behave in this meeting. Below is a list with suggestions you can pick from. Normally we set three to five ground rules.

- Turn on video.
- Mute when listening.
- Only mute when needed.

- We participate actively during the session.
- We respect time (we start and end on time).
- We respect each other's perspectives.
- We singletask (don't multitask).
- We ask questions by... e.g. raising a hand, writing in the chat.
- We challenge perspective by asking questions first.
- We appoint a meeting facilitator.
- We appoint a person who is capturing notes from the meeting.

Figure 17.2 shows an example of how such rules could look like on a slide.

> *Top tip: If you are having recurring meetings you could consider creating the ground rules together – that makes it far more likely that people will follow them, and it's also easier to refer back to them when participants feel ownership.*

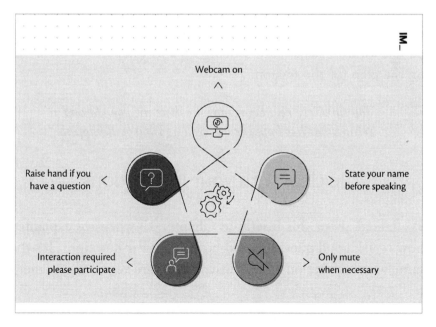

Figure 17.2   Examples of ground rules

Apart from presenting ground rules for the meeting another way to be proactive in creating a shared idea of how you'll work together could be to frame the session mentally. This means that you illustrate what sort of mindset you expect people to enter the session with today. This could be 'No limitations today' or 'We need to reach a decision before 10.00'. In the moment, a short framing as well as specific timeboxing of exercises of elements can be useful. Finally, reactive actions are to hold people accountable for the ground rules, such as reacting to people not being back on time or turning the camera on. Beware of creating too much negative energy doing this, yet make sure they know to stop it at an early stage and prevent a bad meeting culture to flourish.

Use the agenda actively during the session

If you were in a physical room you would have the agenda displayed on the wall, for instance. In a virtual session that's not possible. Therefore you need to repeatedly go back to the agenda. Each time you move on to another point on the agenda, make people aware that you are moving on and what stage you are at on the plan for the session.

> *Top tip: Give regular recaps. Look at the agenda and recap what has happened as well as what will happen.*

Be clear with your instructions

We talked about this briefly in Chapter 12 when we explained how to ask good questions and how to answer questions. It's the same with instructions. Clear instructions are key to engagement and results, not only in terms of being clear about what the question is, but also how you want participants to respond to it.

We recommend using slides to visualise the instructions and make it easier for you as a facilitator to be very clear. It can be very easy to think that if you just say it out loud people will get it – we have seen too often that this does not work. It's far more effective to have a visual representation of your instructions to support the visual cortex of the brain. Have the question written on a slide, as well as how you want them to engage with that question. It needs to be crystal clear for people so that they are in no doubt about what you are asking them to do and what output they are expected to produce.

Figure 17.3 shows an example of how to set up a slide that provides clear instructions for your participants.

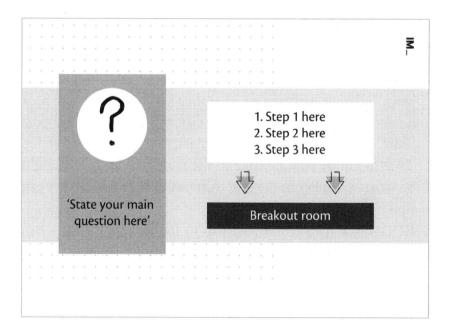

Figure 17.3   Give clear instructions to the participants

There are four steps to setting up instructions:

1. Cue the instructions: This is really important. Lead into your instructions with a phrase like, 'When I've finished explaining it, you will do the following.' This primes people to really listen because they know an exercise is coming up and they will be expected to do something. Always using the same design for your instruction slides can be a useful visual cue for you and the participants, to stage that you need to listen carefully for the instructions so you know what to do.

2. Give clear instructions: This is where you state your main question/task and make sure it has a clear purpose and that it's clear what you will be resolving through this question/task. You also need to explain clearly how you will solve this question or exercise. On the example slide (Figure 17.3), you'll see that we have steps 1, 2 and 3, but you don't necessarily need three steps. One might be sufficient. Only write the information that is necessary here; don't fill the slide with text that isn't important.

3. Explain what participants should do when they finish or need help: Tell your participants what they need to do to come back once they've completed the exercise. Give them a clear time limit and tell them how they can ask for help if they need it. That might be coming back to the main meeting, or it might be writing a query in the chat. Also tell people where they can find help if they need it.

4. Release the instruction: Be sure to make it very clear when the exercise will start. You can say, 'Three, two, one, go!' or 'I've set the timer and you've got five minutes, go!' It's important that people know when the exercise has started and when you've finished giving instructions.

Remind people of the instructions

When you are sending people away from the main virtual space, into breakout rooms for example, make sure that they are able to refer back to the instructions you just gave them. We are sometimes quite surprised at how fast participants (and we ourselves) forget what they have just heard and have completely different conversations to the ones you planned for. It's helpful to provide your participants with a template to fill in when you are sending them off to do exercises like this. This can also create a little push to fill it out, being productive during the session. A good tip is to include the instructions at the top of any shared documents you are getting your participants to work on, so that they have the same instructions they just saw on your slide to refer back to. Or you could send them a link in their breakout rooms to allow them to access these instructions easily. Figure 17.4 is an example of an instruction for an entire process.

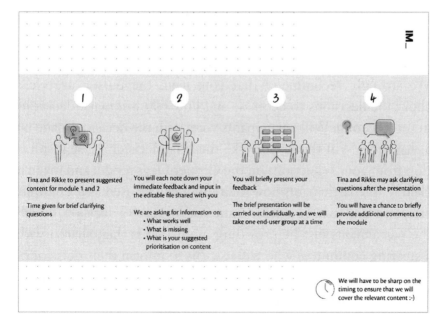

Figure 17.4   Taking participants through the whole process

Tips to create clarity during breakouts

- Give people a template or framework to help them focus on the task.

- Get one person in each team to act as the team leader or facilitator to take care of this process – you can assign someone or ask the team to decide among themselves.

- Give one person responsibility for sharing the key learnings from their team's discussions – this is important to prevent the awkward silence when you come back to plenary.

- Be clear about how long the breakout will last and who will keep track of time.

Be clear about how you take decisions and what they look like

We strongly recommend that you, from the outset, are clear about the decisions to be made and how you will make decisions in this meeting. Will participants vote, with the decision made by a majority? Will the leader take the final decision? Use inspiration from your reflections on the Corner Flags model and make it clear to the participants how their input will be used. For example, are you going to have a democratic vote to reach a decision, or will the participants just be providing input that is then shared with a steering committee who will use this to inform their decision?

The other aspect to this is how you cement the decisions. You need to make sure that you document the decisions that are made. Visualising this, using a whiteboard or a shared document, is useful because it can make everything that you're talking about more concrete, and clearer for those in the session.

You can also replay each decision at the end of the meeting, or at set points throughout, where someone talks through the decision to ensure it is aligned with what was discussed among all the participants. This can then all go into the minutes of the meeting so that everyone has a clear record of what decisions were taken and why.

Three simple steps to help overcome the confusion of being lost in a virtual meeting

1. Frame what is about to happen and what you want to talk about.
2. Do it.
3. Recap what you have done and what has been decided.

18

Connect the Dots

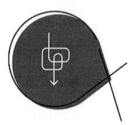

Figure 18.1

When you're on an aeroplane and you're coming in to land, you start really high up with a good perspective of things. You're looking at the world from above and seeing the bigger picture. You can see the main roads, the forests and the full coastline. As you come closer to the ground, you trade this wide perspective for a more detailed view, where you can see small houses, cornfields or the white tops of the waves in the ocean. The closer you get to landing, the more detail you're able to see of what's on the ground.

Your job as the facilitator is to fly your participants into the session, starting high in the air and gradually coming to land the plane. Remember to think about your participants. They probably haven't spent the past few days looking at the context and content of the session like you have, so you need to help them through by drawing the bigger picture. It's your responsibility to tell them why your session is important and why you are doing each step in the process.

This isn't just about flying them into the session, but about helping them to zoom out to make sense of your session, and making it relevant to them. Often we expect people to be able to do this for themselves, but always remember that if your participants are involved in more things than just your session, they will probably need more help than you think is necessary. As the facilitator, you have to help them by creating meaning and telling the story.

In the last chapter we talked specifically about creating clarity at various points within a session. In this chapter what we're talking about is making sure that all your participants have a general understanding of the topic of the session and how that's connected to the wider context. We like to describe it as sense-making. If the session doesn't make sense to your participants then there is a much greater chance that they won't engage with it and you won't reach your goal.

Yet a flight doesn't end when you land the aeroplane. It continues when you disembark. It's the same with your session. When you're connecting the dots, you're bringing in that thread that ties all the elements of your session together, linking it to what's happened before and what is going to happen after.

If this is part of a series of meetings, you need to show the path between the different sessions. So, you've landed your participants in one destination, they have a couple of weeks to look around and then you'll see them on the next flight on the way to the next destination.

You might also need to talk about how this relates to other projects that are happening, or how it relates to your participants' daily work. If you think of the previous chapter – about creating clarity – as helping people to understand the detail on each of the pieces of a jigsaw puzzle, this chapter is about how you then put those pieces together to make one big picture.

Answer the 'Why?' question (a lot!)

Answering 'Why?' should be part of a process of sense-making throughout your session. You need to answer the 'Why?' question for your participants at the beginning, but you also need to think about sense-making for each point of the agenda or exercise.

Some of the questions you could answer at the beginning of a session are:

- Why are we together?
- Why should we spend more time on this?
- What is the end goal?
- Where are we in the overall process?
- What does the big picture look like?
- Why are we meeting again? (If you previously had a session or sessions.)

It's important that you frame each exercise by answering this particular 'Why?', because your participants themselves might be wondering, 'Why are we doing this?' Just because it makes sense to you, that doesn't mean it will also make sense to them. Explain whether each exercise is for fun, to engage with a topic, or to energise everyone. Whatever the reason you have put that exercise into your plan, make sure you share it with your participants.

If people don't understand why you're asking them to do something, they might become annoyed, have resistance to an exercise or simply disengage from the session.

> *Top tip: During the session when you're running activities, make sure you answer this question: Why are we doing this activity? Tell people explicitly: 'The reason we're doing this activity is because. . .'*

When you're in a training or learning situation, think about how you can connect the things that you're learning with previous examples, or to future learning and uses. Ideally, relate what you're teaching your participants to their personal past or future experiences. If you can do this, it's more likely your participants will remember what you teach them.

Another way to help your participants to learn is to share what you have taken from an exercise. Hearing about your own and others' learning can help reinforce a concept or point in your participants' minds.

As a facilitator, you can consider involving participants in the sense-making by asking them to make sense of it themselves and put it into a context that's relevant to them. Such as:

- How does this idea/solution/xxx make sense to you?
- How would X/Y/Z be relevant in your tasks?

Finally, at the end of the session, it's effective to continue the sense-making and connect the dots to what will happen next. Here is a suggestion for questions to answer at the end:

- What did we do?
- Why did we do this?
- What were your inputs good for?
- What will happen next?

The following are the beginnings of some sentences that you could use to help you connect the dots and explain the 'Why?' behind the session:

- Last time we met, we worked with. . .
- Today we will work with. . .
- This is important because. . .
- What we're aiming for is. . .
- The reason we're doing this activity is. . .

Top tip: Remember that the purpose of not just your overall session, but the exercises within it, should never be hidden from the participants. Give them that overall view as well as zooming in on the details.

It can be helpful to use speaker notes alongside your PowerPoint slides to remind you to answer the 'Why?' at every stage when you are new to virtual facilitation. You could even include the purpose on your slides, or a point to remind you to explain the purpose to the participants.

From our experience it's very rare that a facilitator will answer the 'Why?' question too much, so don't be afraid of breaking it down and answering 'Why?' for every part of your session. We don't believe you can ask and answer 'Why?' too many times!

End sessions on a high

Often we find that facilitators can get a bit stressed towards the end of their sessions. However, you should be aware that the last 15 minutes of your session are important in terms of the experience of your participants. It's also an opportunity for you as the facilitator to take something away from it.

We know from several studies by Daniel Kahneman[1] about how the way our brains work – that after an experience people tend to remember the peaks of an experience, as well as the end of the experience. It's really important that you add value at the end of the meeting and that you end your session in the right way.

A key element of the end of a session is to make sure you agree what was decided and how this will be taken further. You want your participants to feel like something has happened during the session, and that something is going to happen as a result of what you've done. You want them to leave the meeting feeling that it was worthwhile, and confident that you will take their input further, or that they have a chance to take their own input further.

You need to bring as much energy to the end of the session as you have throughout the rest of the session.

One way to wrap up a session is using a closer, as we described in Chapter 10 in Part II. Make sure that you have some good questions at the end to help the participants consolidate their learning or to make them excited about what they've done in your session. That might be asking what their key takeaway was, what they enjoyed most about the process, what their next steps should be, or what three things they learned about themselves. The message is not only to take the opportunity to consolidate, but also to get feedback.

---

[1]Kahneman, Daniel (2000). 'Evaluation by moments, past and future' (PDF). In Kahneman, Daniel; Tversky, Amos (eds.). *Choices, Values and Frames*. Cambridge University Press. p. 693.

The reason it's so important to ask for feedback at this stage is that this is an opportunity to find out whether it was a successful session. If you don't ask your participants how it was for them at this point, there's a good chance you will close your virtual meeting and be wondering whether you succeeded and whether it was a good meeting. Or that participants will forget to reply on your survey afterwards.

There are many simple ways that you can ask for that feedback, whether it's opening up a question in the chat, or even running a poll to ask what people were excited about. If your participants leave the meeting feeling excited, you should also have the same feeling. You need to know what you did well and whether you achieved the purpose.

When you ask for feedback at the end, think about how you ask for feedback. You want to spread positive energy. Don't ask, 'Did I do well?', instead ask, 'What worked well?' Remember what we talked about in relation to asking open questions. Also be prepared, if something didn't work as planned, for people to bring this up. You will already know this, so try to frame your question in a way that gets the participants to focus on the positives of the session. We'll take a closer look at feedback in Part IV, talking about 'after'.

Top tip: If possible, and it fits the purpose, you could end your session with a surprise. It might be a screenshot of all the participants while they were working, or a little video that makes them smile from the session, or even just a fun GIF. You want to have a good ending, something that your participants are not quite prepared for, that will just pick up the excitement levels at the end. Be creative!

19

Wrapping Up the During Part

Now that you've finished reading about the 'during' part, you'll hopefully have realised that there are a lot of things to be aware of during a virtual session. The more skilled you become as a facilitator, the easier it becomes to juggle all the different things you need to be aware of. Our best advice is to start training right away, because the more experience you get, the better you get.

This phase also demonstrates why you need to be very firm and thorough with your planning, because the more you have planned, the more free you are to handle what's going on in a session. As we said before, if you have the luxury, you could consider assigning a co-facilitator and/or tech assistant to help you with this job.

Below is a table with an overview of some of the things we think you could benefit from remembering from the during phase. Don't try to do everything at once; pick one thing to focus on. Select what you think is most important for you and go from there.

Chapter	Top takeaways
14: Be On Top	• Be there in good time before the session starts.
	• Be on top of the process by knowing your playbook.
	• Decide and agree on how to communicate if you have a co-facilitator and tech assistant.
	• Know the tech setup you use and how to troubleshoot.
	• Do a 'tour de platform' at the beginning of the session if participants are new to it.
	• Frame your role at the start and get permission from the group to be the facilitator.
	• Know your role through the session, and communicate it to participants, especially if it changes (e.g. from facilitator to expert).
15: Engage the Participants	• Involve all participants during the first ten minutes of the session (breakout, chat and so on).
	• Ensure everyone knows why and 'what's in it for me'.
	• Use micro-involvements to ensure engagement.
	• Believe in the process yourself to make people follow you.
	• Ask good questions and have a process around this that invites engagement.

Chapter	Top takeaways
16: Manage the Energy	• Think about what sort of energy you need for your session – and how to create this.
	• Play music that supports the energy.
	• Be the host. Make small talk, say welcome to people, smile, relax.
	• Use your voice and body language strategically.
	• Be aware of people's attention span in virtual meetings. After 10 minutes their attention starts to drop, so use micro-involvements.
	• Have breaks of around 7 minutes every 45–60 minutes.
	• Use energisers to move and recharge energy.
17: Create Clarity	• Create clarity about the process. Tell people where you are in the process and where you are going next using the agenda.
	• Create a shared idea of how you will work together using ground rules – and enforce them in a nice way.
	• Create clarity about how people can contribute. Remove the social barriers we often encounter in the virtual space.
	• Visualise your instructions in a clear way.
	• Timebox exercises in breakout rooms.
	• Tell people what is about to happen and recap what you decided/did.
	• Create clarity about decision-making. Explain what decisions you will make and who will make them. Set expectations in the beginning. During the meeting, recap what decisions were made.

Chapter	Top takeaways
18: Connect the Dots	• Answer the 'Why?' question (a lot!). • Make sense around your session – describing the bigger perspective as well as the details. • Give people a chance to consolidate their takeaways. • Close the session on a high.

IV

After – Start Implementing

To ensure you get the full effect from your session, it's important to remember that it doesn't end when the participants have left the meeting. This isn't only about learning for yourself as the facilitator, or for the organisation. You should keep your stakeholders or participants in the loop and remind them of what you talked about, what you decided or what the next step in the process is. The after phase is where we see the behaviour change or business impact of the meeting. As the facilitator it's your job to follow up with your participants.

In this phase there are a couple of things that are important. It's important for you to evaluate the session and it's important for you to follow up with your participants by giving out any material or sharing any relevant information afterwards. Finally, it's important to use the inputs to continue with your project if this is relevant.

Ideally you will plan the follow-up when you're in the before phase designing the session. You need to think about how you will follow up with participants and also when you can put that into your calendar so that you make time for it. Otherwise there is a danger that you'll focus on conducting a high-quality session but forget about what happens next.

What we find is that the longer it takes for you to do the follow-up after a session, the more work you need to do to produce the follow-up. If you leave it too long then you can lose momentum. This part of the book is about how you can keep the good energy, vibe and progress going after the meeting.

It's also about how you can develop your skills as a facilitator. If you think about this in terms of running sessions in the physical world, you might talk to the participants after the meeting, or you might meet your participants at the coffee machine in the following days and talk about the session. If you're truly virtual and your participants are spread across the world, you won't meet. These opportunities to gather informal feedback and to follow up won't occur. That's why it's so important to plan your evaluation and to follow up a virtual session, because you don't have as many informal touchpoints and it's important to demonstrate progress clearly, whether you do that in an email, on a collaboration platform or in some other format.

20

Feedback and Evaluation

Figure 20.1

Evaluation is about looking critically at the session, at the end or shortly afterwards, in terms of the design and the facilitation. This will help you to learn and grow as a facilitator and demonstrates that you care about the quality of your sessions. To do this you should be curious about what worked very well and what you can improve for next time. We believe that it's very important that you don't come out of the meeting and only trust your own feeling about how it went. It's important to collect data and ask for perspectives from others. Those might come from other members of the planning team (if there are any) and/or the participants. Without this input, it can be difficult to find out what was effective.

Evaluation and feedback are always an opportunity to learn and grow, even though it can feel unpleasant to ask for feedback. Especially if you are new to virtual facilitation, feedback can help you to keep the good elements in your session and also give you an idea of what's not working. Even as an experienced facilitator there is always more to learn.

The growth mindset is about accepting that as humans we can always learn and develop. You might not be naturally good at something, so if you need to master this space in terms of becoming a virtual facilitator, know that it can take effort. You will make a lot of mistakes and you need to come away from them with the view that they are lessons. Be aware of what everyone else does in this area. Ask what the best people out there are doing and explore how you can mirror them. Always ask yourself, 'How can I make sure this is one step better next time?' We're not saying you should or will master everything in one go. It's about growing consistently and always looking for your next point of focus. This goes for all the suggestions in this book. You won't master everything during your first session. Start where it makes sense for you and keep a growth mindset to add new things along the way.

Even if you are a skilled facilitator, you should still have this growth mindset and accept that there will still be things you can learn, especially in a virtual space.

It's also important to remember that when we do receive feedback, we naturally have a negative bias. That means we take value from the negative comments and often overlook the positives. Yet we know that we also learn a lot from knowing what works and what to keep doing, so don't forget to ask for this.

How to gather feedback and evaluation

Feedback and evaluation can be carried out in many ways. There is no one method that works best, but we have compiled some suggestions to help you get started.

Select the target of your feedback: It's important to know what you want participants to provide feedback on. Do you want to get feedback on yourself as the facilitator, on the session itself, or on the design of the session? These are the areas that we suggest you start with, but it might be that you want feedback on something completely different. Whatever you want, you need to start by defining it. The feedback could be general, within one of these headlines, to get an idea on the overall impression. You could also select something specific to focus on, like your ability to create engagement during the session. This might be relevant if you have this as a focus area and want to know how you are doing.

Decide who you would like feedback from: As we've already said, your own thoughts and reflections might not be enough. It's always good to start by giving yourself feedback and then put this into perspective by asking others. Think about who are the obvious people to start with, or anyone you would especially like to get feedback from, such as someone you could learn from or an important stakeholder. Do you have a co-facilitator? Could you ask your participants, either in the chat at the end of the session, with a survey or in person? Did you have a planning team and could you ask them? You also need to think about how you can ask for this feedback.

> *Top tip: If you want to improve your skills as a virtual facilitator then, after you've read this book, we strongly advise you to take every opportunity you can, every*

*time you run a session, to get feedback. Actively seek it
out, because we can all learn. Even people with many
years of experience can be inspired by those with an
outside perspective.*

Consider what sort of feedback you want: If you don't really
want feedback then you probably won't listen to it and, if you
don't listen to it, then you won't learn anything or change your
behaviour. Think about whether you have time for long, thorough feedback. Is it really important to get this learning perspective? Or would you prefer shorter or more focused feedback?

Below you will find two examples of how you can take a
structured look at different elements of your session. It might be
that you're curious about the design of the session, in which case
follow the Design Star. Or it might be that you're curious about
your own facilitation skills, in which case follow the Good Virtual Facilitator model (see Part III). If you're new and ambitious
you could go for both. But if you have less time or are working
on something very specific then select one.

Both of the models below encourage you to rate yourself
or the session on a scale of one to five. Have discussions with
the other people involved in planning and designing the meeting about what the scores should be. Or have these discussions
with a sponsor or a client. While you could do this on your own
as the facilitator, it's best to get some outside perspectives as
well. It might be useful to run through this exercise yourself and
then ask for input from others. For some of the elements, such
as the platform, you might be able to use comments that your
participants made in the chat during the session to help gauge
your score.

The Design Star

The Design Star model can be used as a structured way – not only to plan, but also to evaluate the design of your session. Gather your selected feedback group and use the Design Star that we shared with you in the before phase of the book. Rate the design on a scale of one to five based on the first questions, where 1 is Low degree, 3 is neutral and 5 is High degree, and discuss your scores based on these further questions.

- **Purpose:** To what degree did we reach the purpose and our success criteria? _____
  - What did we not succeed with? What do we need to cope with this?
- **Participants:** To what degree did we have the right participants in the room? _____
  - Was anyone missing? Was anyone not needed?
- **Platform:** To what degree did the platform work as planned? _____
  - Should we use the same platform next time?
- **Process:** To what degree did the process work with our participants? _____
  - What can we learn about the process for next time?
- **Partners:** To what degree did the partnering work during the session? _____
  - Where did we have – or miss – the right partners? Were they played in the right way?

Discuss the scores you have settled on with the group you selected for feedback. Place particular focus on what should be done differently next time. Don't spend much time dwelling on the things that did not go as planned.

The Facilitation Model

The Good Virtual Facilitator model can be used as another way of evaluating the session by looking not on the design and plan, but on the very facilitation of your session. Gather your selected feedback group and use the five elements from the during phase of the book to assess your performance as the facilitator. It's really important to get an outside perspective for this model because it's very difficult for you to see how you come across during a session. Rate the facilitation on a scale of one to five, where 1 is Low degree, 3 is neutral and 5 is High degree, and discuss your scores.

- **Be On Top:** To what degree did we handle the process? To what degree were we on top of the tech side of the session? To what degree were we on top of the content?

- **Engage the Participants:** To what degree did we manage to create involvement? To what degree did we manage to create variation?

- **Manage the Energy:** How was the general atmosphere in the room? To what degree did we feel fully present and come across with the right energy for the session? To what degree did we manage to handle the participants' energy?

- **Create Clarity:** To what degree did we make it clear to the participants what to do and how to contribute? To what degree did we make it clear to the participants what their role was in the decision-making process? To what degree did we make it clear to participants what was decided? To what degree did we make it clear to participants what the next steps and actions would be?

- **Connect the Dots:** To what degree did we create meaning around the process? To what degree did we connect the before and the after to the meeting?

Discuss the scores you have settled on with the group you selected for feedback. Place particular focus on what you should keep doing and do differently next time. Don't spend much time dwelling on the things that did not go as planned.

How to get the most from feedback

Very few of us like to get feedback if all we're being given is a list of things we should do differently or improve. For most people that is really hard to listen to. While some have a high tolerance for it, most of us need to have our feedback served up to us in a smarter way to enable us to take it in and act on it.

We know from the science of the brain that you get more of the things that you focus on.[1] Firstly, when you talk about feedback, we would very much encourage you to put most of the focus on the things that you want to get more of or that you want to start doing. Don't spend too much time on the things that didn't work.

> *Top tip: When working with feedback look forwards rather than backwards.*

As you're working through the models, consider the concept of Keep, Start, Stop Doing as illustrated in Figure 20.2.

---

[1]Research on self-directed neuroplasticity, Dr. Jeffrey M. Schwartz, http://jeffreymschwartz.com/

Keep	Stop	Start
Note what to keep	Note what to stop	Note what to start
1.	1.	1.
2.	2.	2.
3.	3.	3.
4.	4.	4.
5.	5.	5.
6.	6.	6.

Figure 20.2   Keep, stop, start

- Is there anything you should start doing?
- Is there anything you should stop doing?
- And is there anything you should continue doing?

Look at what worked so that you strengthen and continue doing that. Then look at what you need to do more of. Don't focus on what you should stop doing. These might sound similar, but reframing it has a huge impact in terms of the likelihood of you making a change.

Another way to approach feedback is to look at two questions:

1. What went well?
2. What could be improved?

This will encourage you to look at the improvements you can make rather than looking at what didn't work.

These are just a few suggestions as to how you can approach feedback in a constructive way to give yourself the best chance of listening to it and learning from it.

Five minutes of feedback for the facilitator: how to do this in practice in a virtual meeting

1. **Ask for participants to provide feedback for you.**

2. **Tell what you want feedback on**: The facilitator should set the scene for what to provide feedback on. It can be based on a general impression, the themes in the model of the Design Star or the Good Facilitator, or something specific that they are working on. If you have five minutes to use for this, you'll learn a lot.

3. **Be clear about how you would like the feedback**: Do you want to know about what went well or do you want to know what could be improved? And how should participants provide it? You can use a small poll or ask for inputs in the chat or Menti. If you use a poll or Menti the feedback will be anonymous which can sometimes make people more honest.

4. **Say thank you for the feedback**: Don't start discussing it in plenary.

This is a fast and efficient way to get opinions.

If you get a comment that you don't understand and are curious about, you can get back to it afterwards. Either ask the participant to elaborate or ask one of the participants that you know well how they see it. We always suggest being curious rather than defensive to learn the most.

Remember that feedback is based on the opinion of the individual – it's subjective and, as such, the statement of one participant is not necessarily the truth about how the session was perceived generally.

Although you can ask people for feedback after the session, they are much more likely to provide it if you do it at the end of the session than if you wait until after they have left the virtual meeting.

You'll find some examples of different feedback surveys that you can use in your sessions in our online resources. www.implement.dk/vf#methods

Giving feedback to the participants

Sometimes, as the facilitator, you may need to give some feedback to your participants about how they behaved in the meeting. You may not need to give feedback to everyone, but there might be a few individuals you want to start some dialogue with. It might be that they didn't have the right energy in the session, that they didn't do something or were resistant to exercises. This is especially important in recurring meetings and other touchpoints that you have on an ongoing basis, or if you are a team leader.

For example, if you're hosting a team meeting and one person is being really engaged and active on the chat, you could go back to them afterwards and offer them some appreciative feedback on the way they participated in the meeting. By starting that dialogue, they may also give you feedback.

You also need to take responsibility for the future quality of meetings, as well as for your own learning. For example, if someone isn't engaging or is behaving in a disruptive way, you will want to find a sensitive way to address that behaviour. In a physical setting, you might go over to them during a break and say, 'Anna, could I ask you to just rethink how you're being in this meeting and what is standing in your way?' But in a virtual meeting you won't have this opportunity for that offline calibration. As a virtual facilitator, that leaves you with the difficult task of maybe guiding, coaching, nudging or pushing the right behaviour.

The other people you may want to give feedback to are the partners in your meeting.

How to share feedback with others

You could use the feedback model shown in Figure 20.3 to give feedback to others. Our approach to feedback is based on four elements – the four Cs.

- Curious
- Caring
- Concrete
- Constructive

Figure 20.3   Example of a feedback model

Curiosity is a very effective way of giving feedback. Instead of saying, 'I think what you did was bad' you can ask, 'I'm curious, can you tell me about why you did that?' This can open their ears and get them to listen because you start a dialogue around the feedback. You might also learn something!

Caring feedback is feedback that is delivered with empathy and the aim to help another. Being caring in the feedback means to focus both on the positive things and on the things to improve, with a nice balance between the two of them. We recommend not necessarily stating everything you noted, as that can be overwhelming and ineffective as the ears of the receiver often close. Consider what would be most helpful for the receiver to know. What would be the next step from your point of view? Start with this and wait with the rest for next time.

Concrete feedback is feedback that you can learn from. It's always nice to hear that you 'facilitated a session well' or that you 'did a good job'. That probably creates a nice feeling and makes you happy and satisfied. Yet it's quite difficult from this to know what you actually did, that made it a well-facilitated session. Was it the way you used exercises, created engagement or provided clarity around decisions? If you don't get specific information on what was especially appreciated, you basically don't get any knowledge about why the session was perceived as 'well facilitated' or what you should keep for the next session. Provide concrete feedback, by telling what you *observed* and how it made *you* feel. 'I noted that we were sent into breakout rooms several times during the session. This provided me with an intimate room to have deeper and engaging conversations and even though it was a two-hour session it felt so short.' Providing this sort of feedback is concrete and something the receiver can learn a lot from.

Constructive refers to the type of feedback you provide. It can be very helpful to look at the parts to improve, but make sure you do it in a way that fosters learning instead of a mental block out. Our approach would be to look more at what we want more of, than what we don't like. This is not to say that you shouldn't tell what you observed, and how this made you feel, but from there be constructive. Go into suggestions on alternatives and spend the time exploring these. 'I noted that you were the only one talking during the entire session using a PowerPoint with a lot of slides and text. I really tried to keep focus and concentration, but after 15 minutes I simply couldn't keep focus any more and by now I don't remember much of what was said. It would help me a lot to stay focused if the session could be a little more interactive – maybe with a short question or small poll. If you would like to explore this together let me know.'

Always remember that feedback is subjective. One person's experience of a session may not be the same as another person's experience in the same session. It's important to be aware of this and to deliver your feedback in a way that isn't accusatory, but that tells the receiver what you *observed*, what this made *you* feel, or if it gave *you* an idea on something to do more of, or change, for example.

21

Follow Up

Following up with the participants in your session is important to ensure that your session has the desired impact and effect. You always need to remember that even if you had a great meeting, it doesn't end when you hit the 'End meeting' button. To really succeed with a project, change people's behaviour or encourage them to take action, you need to give them friendly reminders and make this follow-up visual and easy. As the facilitator, this is part of your job.

You probably have a plan in your head about what you want people to do next, but if you don't communicate that to your participants or follow up with them, this will be like a black box. They won't know what's going on inside. Following up is a way to open that black box, to help make sense of what you're asking of them and to encourage them to act, contribute or whatever else you need them to do.

Design for follow-up

Following up is a big part of the design and is something you should think through from the start. We've seen the most successful workshops and meetings, but then afterwards nothing changes or people don't follow through on what they committed to. Usually this is because the facilitator hasn't planned to follow up. As a facilitator, it's your job to design a relevant follow-up where you engage the right people, at the right level, after the session.

What does a good follow-up look like?

A good follow-up should be visual, short, should recommend action and be a way of creating clarity in terms of what comes next. It should motivate people and make them feel as though they want to continue doing what they set out to do in your session. It's also an opportunity to reinforce the sense-making aspect of your session and put it into the broader context. Remind people about your purpose.

When we talk about following up, we mean that you create a feeling of importance around the time spent in the meeting and the value added. You can do this by sharing the decisions that were made or the materials that were used or created in the session, but also by recapping the feeling or atmosphere in the session if this was special. You're also following up on the meeting in terms of the visual output, or decisions, and ensuring that people know what to do next.

When we're talking about following up virtually, it is very easy to find yourself following up with an email. An email is fine, you can do a lot with that, but being in a virtual space you might also want to consider using a platform or communication channel that you used during the session.

> *Top tip: If you had the opportunity to have a chat or channel, please continue using it. This can also make your follow-up more interactive.*

The virtual space allows for easy visual asynchronous interaction. This means that participants can interact on a platform such as Teams after the meeting using posts to get updated and continue the dialogue. This is an easy opportunity to do an active follow-up and keep participants and stakeholders in the loop. Tell them that you'd like to hear their opinion about something specific. Ask them what progress they're making or whether they'd like to share what they've been doing since the meeting. Encourage them to post and share important information, or share your own progress on the work cut out to make the platform relevant. Appropriate content is not the only important matter; keep in mind that it is very important that you pick the right platform for your follow-up activities, because you want to make sure that it's a platform that people like and find easy to use.

Again, this is something you should consider in the design phase. The reason it's so important to plan your follow-up is that you want to remove as many barriers as possible to people doing it.

When to follow up

There are different points at which you may want to follow up with your participants.

Immediately

This means that the follow-up should appear for the participants within 24 hours of the session ending. If you wait until after 24 hours have passed, there is a much greater chance of them hitting the 'forgetting curve' and just getting on with something else.

Below we created a list describing the actions we typically do as a part of the follow-up.

- Follow up on your session with the co-facilitator, design team and the participants.
- Share materials, contact information and an action list. Make sure people know what was decided and what they need to do. Be very clear on deadlines and when they can expect to hear from you again or what the next touch-point will be.
- If your session was about creating energy for a change or a new idea, consider sharing something that demonstrates that energy during the session. You might have made a word cloud, a recording of an energiser or something fun – be creative! Positive emotions help you move forward.

It's really important that you don't delay your immediate follow-up by more than 24 hours. If people have the motivation and want to do something, you don't want to be the barrier by failing to give them access to the materials they need.

> *Top tip: Do this follow-up as fast as possible. You want to make this accessible. It's also a great chance for you to show that you welcome feedback.*

Some people will feel as though they want to hold back their slides. Before a session this can be a good way of generating curiosity and suspense, but once you have finished the session we would recommend sending your slides out to the participants. Remember that people can record virtual sessions, so if they want your material they will usually be able to get access to it. That's why we recommend sending out your slides, but as a PDF to ensure they stay in the right order.

If you don't want to share all of your slides because not everything is relevant after the session, you can select a package of the most important things and send those out so that everyone has a nice reminder of the core content.

If there are legal reasons why you may not want to share your slides, for instance because they contain business-sensitive information, you could share them in a virtual space that has restricted access.

You can also go for just a one-pager if you want. It could be the action list, pieces of advice, or the things that the participants committed to. Usually less is more here.

If you have recorded the session, it is usually a good idea to share this as well, because then people who had to leave the session early, either because of technical issues or because they couldn't stay for the duration due to other commitments, can catch up. They'll find it valuable. If you don't have a recording of the whole session but only parts, make sure you provide context around them when you share them. It's also important to note that you need to tell your participants at the time that you will be recording the session and ask their permission to share it afterwards.

If you are sharing a recording of your session, think about where you will share it. Do you share it on YouTube where everyone can access it, or do you share it via a locked channel that is password protected?

Medium term

What medium term means in relation to meeting follow-ups will very much depend on the type of session. If it's a recurring meeting, you would follow up between sessions, but if it's a workshop then you'll approach the follow-up differently. The point is that you should follow up according to what makes sense for your session.

Generally, we would say you should start your medium-term follow-up three days to a week after your session. During that space of time it's still fresh in everyone's mind but people will have had the opportunity to do some work.

Although you want to make the first follow-up within a week, this medium-term phase can stretch to three weeks. It might be that you need to organise another meeting to make a decision, or that there needs to be another meeting that doesn't involve the same participants. But to move things forward you need to keep communicating and showing everyone that you're moving onto the next step. You can't always wait until the next step arrives.

The key is fighting the 'forgetting curve'. You will have a dramatic fall on the 'forgetting curve' within the first six days. That means you need to send some kind of reminder within the first week if you want something to happen.

Although we often talk about the 'forgetting curve' from a learning perspective, at this stage it is also true in relation to feeling involved and that you are able to make a difference. It's about maintaining the impact that your session has over the medium term.

It's important that your participants know whether what they did in the session made a difference, and whether their input was used. If you don't communicate that to them then they are likely to be left feeling as though their involvement was a waste of their time. On the other hand, don't just follow up for the sake of it. Use people's time wisely and ensure your effort creates value for the project and those involved.

We would also suggest following up in the medium to long term with your co-facilitators, the design team and the participants. This kind of follow-up would be a 'Where are we now?' type of message. It might be that you do this two weeks after a session or even a month after.

In this follow-up, you should explain what happens now. Tell the participants how their inputs and decisions will be used. It could be that at this stage you know more about how the input from the meeting will be used than you did at the time.

Consider who needs to be involved now and what the next steps are. You should also share the decisions made by the steering committee, if something like this has taken place. This follow-up is all about the things that happened after the session. If you got input for a decision, what was the outcome?

You can also use this follow-up for more practical elements. For example, if we decided that Henrik should do X, Kåre should do Y and Iben should do Z, then, as the facilitator, you might need to give them a friendly reminder if they haven't done it. You could do this by asking about their progress before your next meeting, or you could notify them of deadlines and put placeholders in their calendars. Placeholders are something you might consider in the immediate follow-up, but at the medium-term stage you need to make sure that any commitments that were made during the meeting are followed up by action. It's about holding people responsible for what was agreed on.

As a facilitator, it can be easy to feel as though you're disturbing people, but in our experience people often like to receive these friendly reminders. You have to remember that it's not about you but about helping your participants move forward.

With the medium-term follow-up you may also have a communication task as the facilitator. It's not only about figuring out what happens now, but communicating that to the people who need to know. Hopefully, as the facilitator, you are on top of your project or meeting, but you need to remember that the people around you – the key stakeholders and the participants – won't know that if you don't tell them. Share it, make it mean something to them. You can use a collaboration platform, emails or whatever you feel will best pass on the message that something is going on, something has happened and you are moving forward.

The key with these medium-term follow-ups is that you want to encourage the participants to contribute. Try to make your follow-up a sustainable solution where they can see what's happening, and invite them to share their work, progress and what they're doing. Encourage other people to come up with ideas. If you're the only person who is driving the agenda, it's probably not sustainable in the long run, so consider handing out assignments and invite people to share in your success.

Maintain engagement with key stakeholders. Share the good case studies and progress in a virtual space. Use the opportunities that the virtual world provides. As noted earlier you can use a collaboration platform if you decide that the session requires some kind of follow-up actions or next steps. Use this virtual platform to have discussions. If you use Teams, for instance, you can post what you did, write a quick note and use that platform for asynchronous work. It's not that everyone has to be working at the same time, but in using these virtual collaboration tools you can create the sense that something is happening. This is a good way to help people continue working together in the medium term and a nice, inclusive way to keep things moving forward.

> *Top tip: Introduce the collaboration platform in the session. You want your participants to feel comfortable using it before you ask them to use it on their own. This will help remove that entry barrier to continued contribution.*

To guarantee that there is activity in this kind of virtual space, one person needs to take on the responsibility of being the moderator. As the facilitator this will usually fall to you. That means being the first person to get out there and start doing.

Demonstrate what you're looking for so that other people can see that it's okay for them to contribute as well. Be aware that this is an investment for you, where you use your time to ensure engagement and progress in the project. It's really important, as far as possible, to show people what the goods look like, to ask them how they're doing and to follow up and share case studies. If you don't have time for this, your participants probably don't have time either.

> *Top tip: These asynchronous options for collaborating are one of the big benefits to the virtual space, so use them to your full advantage. Make them visual and gather everything in one platform, rather than having lots of emails going back and forth.*

Longer term

There is a significant difference in how long you would follow up for, and what format those follow-ups would take, depending on the type of session that you've run. For example, the kind of follow-up you do for a small recurring meeting will be very different to the follow-up you do for a strategic seminar or workshop.

If you've delivered a major, designed, critical strategic workshop, then the follow-ups may go on for one or two months afterwards, where you're sharing the decisions that are being made by the steering committee and what all the different groups have been doing. If you're having a weekly meeting, then this level of long-term follow-up simply isn't necessary. If you hosted an event with external stakeholders that was sales focused, then the strategy for your follow-up would change again.

Generally, long-term follow-up only really applies to large-scale events or critical strategic workshops and similar sessions.

Don't forget about the benefits of smaller touchpoints

One of the advantages of the virtual space is that it allows us to have smaller touchpoints without a huge investment 'getting there'. It could be a month or so since you last met up, and at this point it might be a good idea to schedule a 15-minute touchpoint meeting. You can use this kind of meeting to check in on where people are with their actions. Having that social commitment of actually meeting up is about changing behaviour. It's also great as a weekly team touchpoint, if you are working apart or from home.

Remember that virtual meetings don't require the same time or energy commitments as physical ones. All the participants can be in completely different places and it won't take them any time to 'travel' to your meeting or cost them any money to get there. This is an opportunity that the virtual world offers that the physical doesn't, and it's one that we should take advantage of.

These kinds of touchpoints don't require a long agenda. All you often need is a short period of time to run through a checklist and allow each person to share their status and how far they've progressed. It's also a chance for people to share whether they need anything to continue.

22

Wrapping Up of Part IV

Now we have been through the after part and we hope it is clear that this phase is where the learning and impact happens for real or fades out. If we don't follow up on the good energy in the session, don't use the input or forget to communicate, the likelihood of something happening is rather low. Hopefully you have in your planning phase already designed the follow-up phase and set aside time to do it – if not, you still have a task at hand.

It is also after the session that you as a facilitator have an opportunity to get feedback and learn what work could be improved or developed for next time.

- Follow up with participants to keep them engaged, in the short, medium and long term.

- Follow up on the project to ensure impact and share progress with participants.

– Ask for feedback from your participants to grow your skills as a virtual facilitator and ensure your sessions provide the impact you are aiming for. If possible do it during the session.

– Provide feedback for participants when needed. Both when you see wanted behaviour and if you need someone to act differently.

V

Deep Dives Into Specific Virtual Formats

We've spent the first four parts of this book looking at virtual facilitation in general. We've explored the process we recommend to use for all sessions and the general mindset you need to step into as a facilitator, as well as a lot of the actions and tools you can use in any kind of session, whether they are small, big, long, short, recurring or one-off. But, of course, there are nuances to the different types of sessions.

In this final part of the book, we would like to highlight some additional elements, tips and tricks for you to be aware of in specific types of virtual sessions. This is a deep dive into five different types of sessions.

The five specific formats we're going to dive into in the coming chapters are:

- Virtual (recurring) meetings
- Hybrid meetings
- Virtual workshops
- Virtual training
- Virtual large-scale events

23

Virtual (Recurring) Meetings

In this deep dive we're going to explore recurring meetings, like stand-up meetings or steering committee meetings. These are meetings that you have regularly, usually with around ten people. They'll normally last between 20 minutes and 1.5 hours as an absolute maximum. This could also apply to departmental meetings where you have 15 to 20 participants.

One thing we often find with these kinds of meetings is that, over time, they can become boring. They need some extra energy or variation injected into them. This is something you need to consider in your planning, and it might be that you need to put a little additional energy in at that stage.

In general, we would say that recurring virtual meetings need to have quite a fast pace to ensure people value them and don't lose enthusiasm. These meetings need to be a place where people receive a very concrete output or alignment and are then able to move forwards. That means, when you go into these meetings, you need to be very clear about what you want to do and what output you're expecting to create.

What happens in recurring virtual meetings shouldn't be a surprise. You should have a very clear vision of how it will work and who will do what. It's particularly crucial that people know the structure and agenda before this kind of meeting. They should go into that meeting knowing exactly what items are on the agenda and what they can expect in terms of their involvement or the output. This can be different to some of the other types of meetings we'll dive into later on.

Be aware that, in a virtual space, these recurring meetings often serve several purposes. They deliver the alignment around the purpose that we just discussed and they deliver clear outputs and actions. But, in a virtual situation, we often aren't sitting with the other participants every day in the same physical space. That means these recurring meetings also serve as a social connection. As such, it's important to make space for that and to give people time to have a short, informal chat.

In recurring meetings, you will generally have the same participants and this allows people to trust each other more. It is likely to make them more comfortable with contributing to discussions and people won't be afraid of talking over someone else, because they know each other. Use that trust and understand how the dynamics will be different in a recurring meeting compared to a one-off meeting.

Before a recurring meeting

We recommend using the principles and ideas we discussed in Part I of the book to prepare yourself for a recurring meeting and the Design Star and playbook from Part II to create a clear design and plan. The good news is that you don't have to do a new design for each session. Make a solid design and plan and reuse this with minor variations.

Before your first meeting (or the next one coming up) spend some time designing and planning. The more times you host the meeting, the more important it is that you have a good design to ensure it's high quality every time. When you are going through the Design Star, consider how often the meeting will recur. Is it a daily stand-up meeting, a weekly departmental meeting or a monthly committee meeting? Generally we have named the period after the meeting 'after'. In recurring meetings it would be more correct to call it 'between'. This both includes following up, but also preparing people for the next session. It's very important to be firm on the process between the meetings in your plan. You need to know what you will do in between meetings to keep the engagement up, as well as what the participants should do. Think about how you will show that things happen not only when you are together, but also when you are apart. Is the meeting only about information or should you use a platform to make inputs or progress visual?

Every three or six months, we would recommend that you reconsider the plan you've created to put some new energy into it. It can also be nice to think of a fun little feature that you can add once in a while. You don't necessarily need to include this element every time, especially if it's a daily meeting, but it is good to have something in mind so that you can bring variation to your sessions.

Remember that virtual meetings don't need to be a circus. You don't need to do something completely new each time. In fact, people prefer to know the structure, to know who has what roles and how the meeting will be run. But you can challenge this a little and change one part to create that excitement or diversity every now and then.

> *Top tip: You don't need to try new things in every recurring meeting. When you've planned a nice format for your recurring meeting it's good to use it! If you're spending less energy on the before phase after your initial planning, it allows you to completely focus on the*

facilitation and effect of the meeting. These meetings
are about efficiency and using your mental energy in
the right place.

Think about how you will manage the energy in your meeting during the design. In recurring meetings you're unlikely to have the same peaks and troughs of energy that you might in a workshop or a large-scale event, but that doesn't mean the whole meeting has to flatline. Consider the small elements you could introduce to pick the energy up a little or introduce variation using the chat, a poll or breakout rooms.

During a recurring meeting

As we mentioned at the start of this chapter, we suggest you make space for people to have social interactions. We recommend allowing five minutes at the beginning of a recurring virtual session to do this. Consider whether it should be voluntary and, if not, remember to set the scene for why and how to make this part of your meeting important for your participants.

As you'll remember from Chapter 15, where we discussed engaging the participants, you need to include regular check-ins with the people in your meeting. In recurring meetings, it can be nice to use one of the following questions as both an opener and a check-in.

- What's been a highlight for you since we talked last?
- What's going on in your space right now?
- What are you looking forward to?
- How are you progressing with the X or Y project?

This is an opportunity to check in with the other participants at the beginning of your meeting – you might even agree to drink coffee together – apart. The formal presentation you would include in a one-off meeting isn't necessary. This informal approach can often open people up and start a dialogue, while creating that social connection and acknowledging that you all know each other. Give people a timeframe of just a couple of minutes to make sure that this part of the session doesn't run over. It's important to facilitate this part of the meeting and give everyone a head's-up when the time is coming to an end.

> *Top tip: Open the meeting room five minutes before the start to give everyone that time to check in and have an informal chat before the formal programme starts. To make this successful, put the start time of the meeting five minutes earlier so that people log in early, or set up a separate appointment called 'warm up' or 'coffee talk'.*

Setting housekeeping rules for your recurring meeting is important. You might have an initial meeting where you decide on these rules, or it might be that through feedback you realise that you need to provide some guidance around housekeeping. When we talk about housekeeping rules in this context, we mean rules of engagement. You need to know how people will show agreement or disagreement in a discussion. Does silence mean that everyone agrees? Should people write in the chat if they disagree? How are we making decisions? These are all questions you should answer with your housekeeping rules.

Suggested rules of engagement for recurring meetings

- Have your webcam on.
- If you agree, click to raise your hand.
- If you disagree, let us know in the chat.
- We start on time and end on time.
- Don't multitask. Close down your emails and phones and be fully present in the meeting.

- Feel free to ask questions along the way.
- Make sure you are located somewhere quiet where you can talk and fully focus on the session.

These rules can be a great way to set out your virtual meeting culture. Just remember that this is only true if you and your participants stick to them. If not, it's your job as the facilitator to enforce them. Consider how best to do this if necessary. Should this be during a session where everybody is present, or is it better to provide feedback to specific participants, either positive or constructive?

Pacing

It's really important to get the pace right in recurring meetings. If the meeting is too long, it becomes boring. If it's too short, people might not follow you or have the chance to contribute. If you are in doubt about whether the pace is right, ask for feedback (and remember that people can often have different opinions or preferences).

Be visual

Another important element in recurring meetings is to make them visual. Visualising makes it easier to talk about the same thing and keep your participants engaged. You can use PowerPoint or collaboration platforms that can be accessed both before, during and after the meeting to visualise your progress, status or whatever is important in your meeting. This can help you stay on top of data and make it easier to follow up and prepare for each session.

Top tips for running an efficient virtual agenda

Use a very easy, collaborative platform where people can work simultaneously. You can even allow five minutes in the meeting itself where each participant adds their notes or comments, or updates the workflow. The key is a platform that is visual and one that you can access on a recurring basis. Figure 23.1 shows an example of a very simple action list from a recurring meeting.

An action list like the one illustrated in Figure 23.1 is a good place to begin and end your virtual recurring meetings if you're not using more advanced collaboration platforms. Use it to guide your agenda.

Action list on meetings				
Nr.	Status	Actions	Responsible	Deadlines

Figure 23.1   A simple action list

After a recurring meeting

It's important that you provide the participants with access to what was agreed during the meeting. Depending on how long you go between meetings, you may also want to reach out to the participants to share progress.

Every three to six months you should evaluate your meeting format. You might want to change it according to the feedback you receive or to provide some new energy and be creative. One of the advantages of recurring meetings is that they are easy to tap into as a participant, but the downside is that over time they can become boring. As we suggested in Part IV, ask your participants for feedback. Every few months ask if they are happy with the way these meetings are running. Do they feel that they're getting boring? Do they want us to tweak them a little bit? You could also consider changing the facilitator to get some new ideas and energy into the meeting.

Facilitating recurring meetings is an excellent opportunity to train your facilitation skills as you get more comfortable with the process and participants to challenge yourself within the art of virtual facilitation. We recommend that you plan for feedback, both from yourself and your participants, to use this opportunity to learn and develop your skills.

> *Top tip: You don't need to reinvent the wheel to keep your recurring meetings fresh and stop them becoming boring. You don't necessarily need to change the format of the meeting. You could introduce a fun fact or comment. You could create an interesting fly-in. You could share a nice observation or something that you did that's important with regards to the meeting. You could add a quick poll. This doesn't need to be more than one or two minutes. Whatever it is, it should be something easy for you to introduce.*

Case: Virtual stand-up meeting to coordinate and distribute tasks in a production team

Purpose	The purpose of the daily morning meeting is to have a dialogue around work distribution.
	In a team the tasks are seldomly distributed evenly. Some can have a lot of tasks while others have little to do. The purpose of the stand-up meeting is a part of an efficient operating system – to coordinate tasks across a team. To get a shared understanding among the leader and the employees of the workload through an informed dialogue. Based on this, tasks and capacity are distributed more evenly in the team to avoid slow case processing or employee burnout due to work overload.
Success criteria	• To ensure transparency in task load in a team.
	• To ensure that workload is equally distributed in a team.
	• To ensure that unequal or high workload is handled.
Participants	An operating team of 5–10 people in a production site that shares a case portfolio.
Platform	Using an online whiteboard with a predefined template and room for data (Excel) in Miro to visualise the planned workload for each worker in the team.
	Visualisation is crucial to create transparency and make the distribution of tasks easy as everyone can see how much work each other has. Some need to work harder – some need to work less hard.
Process	At the end of the day team members update cases produced and their personal case production plan for the following day.
	Each morning a 15-minute meeting, plus 5 minutes for small talk.
	The agenda is the same each day and is followed tightly.
Partners	The leader or a team member facilitates the session.

The solution

10 minutes in the virtual space each morning replaces 30 minutes spent on coordination and firefighting.

A standard agenda, and an online whiteboard interactive template, are crucial to host effective meetings – both with regards to the facilitator's preparation time and the effect of the meeting.

The agenda looks like this:

- Five minutes for informal small talk

- Welcome

- The day yesterday: learnings. Did our effort yesterday call for changes in the plan for today?

- The day today: What do we plan to do? Are there potential challenges? Does someone need help or a talk with the leader?

- Anything we should be aware of going forward?

When the stand-up meeting is purely virtual it becomes THE social routine in a team. This is the only time you meet with colleagues during the day. This is why the social aspect of the meetings becomes important and an opportunity to create motivation in the team. Make room to log in five minutes before the formal session start, tell people about this opportunity and have an open talk to check in with colleagues. If people don't know what to say, have an open question or two such as: what is your most interesting task today?

During Covid-19 many leaders have become positively surprised about the steady productivity despite employees working from home. The stand-up meeting could be hosted as a hybrid meeting, e.g. with 2/3 physically present and 1/3 working from home to accommodate a flexible work situation. Be aware of ensuring that all can see and contribute to the meeting equally.

Virtual recurring meetings are great for a fast team check-in if you're not all sitting in the same office. In the past, everyone would need to physically get together and it took a lot of time. With this virtual format you can take 15 minutes to check in. In our organisation, Implement, we do this on a Monday morning to hear how each person in the team is doing, what they are up to this week and whether there's anything anyone needs help with. Everyone is aligned, have said 'hi' to colleagues and is then ready to go. If you have a distributed team, this is also a great way to create a closer connection between people.

24

Hybrid Meetings

We were in a meeting room with four colleagues, hooked up on Teams, with three more participants distributed around the country. Our focus was on growing our shared sales activities during a 1.5-hour session. In the room we were facing the screen and the host of the session, who was in the meeting room with us. In actual fact, we were facing the back of the host because he was talking to the camera. The host was asking for comments in the chat from the people participating online, which those of us sitting in the room couldn't read or post in because we didn't have our own devices. Also the participants online had trouble hearing what was said from the physical room as the microphone did not catch all our voices. This meeting was not high quality – nor was it very effective.

This is just a brief illustration of how frustrating it can be when you're in a hybrid meeting. We have heard many stories similar to this one and noted how people feel frustrated and/or left out, either because of poor quality sound from the physical room, feeling alone because they are not physically part of 'the group', or due to a lack of connection with the facilitator.

Yet hybrid meetings are the future! There are two reasons for this: first, there are many organisations with a main office, and satellite locations scattered nationally or internationally; second, there are more people working from home to save on the cost of commuting and to give greater flexibility around their working lives. This is why we think this is an important format to look at and improve.

We define a hybrid meeting as a meeting where some participants are physically together in the same room, while others are physically apart. However, everyone is connected via a virtual platform. In this chapter we're going to explore how you can facilitate a meeting where the participants are together in small clusters and collaborating virtually across locations.

The following is our advice for designing and running hybrid meetings.

Before a hybrid meeting

Our key principle when we look at hybrid meetings is to make all the participants equal. You need to design your hybrid meeting to accommodate all the participants. Don't make one or other group feel forgotten or 'second class'. Your setup and process should work just as well for the people in the room with you as those who are participating virtually. Be aware that the people participating virtually can feel more alone or as though they aren't really part of the meeting because of the fact that they are physically disconnected from the others in the group.

Plan for the process to include all participants. This includes ensuring that each person has their own device – including those who are in the room – and an appropriate setup, as discussed in Chapter 4. You especially, as the facilitator, should be aware how you set up your computer if you are present in the room. How are you positioned compared to the other physical participants? Even though you have multiple screens it can be odd not to face each other.

Top tip: In your invitation, be very clear on the fact that participants are expected to be on their own devices, with video turned on.

Design your process to allow for people in the physical room joining online breakouts and collaboration platforms, and be aware that you might have sound issues if the discussions from one person in the physical room can be heard and therefore interfere with one of the other breakout rooms. Think about asking people to have their own earphones as well as their own device or consider using a walk and talk for open discussions in breakout rooms. This also provides some extra energy in the meeting.

If the hybrid meeting is recurring we recommend also reading Chapter 23 about recurring meetings, and use the tips from that. Especially regarding how to design and plan once and then reuse the design.

During the hybrid meeting

Be on top with an appropriate technical setup

One key to success is to have a technical setup that enables you as a facilitator to run the process equally for all participants. Locate your setup (camera, etc.) in a way that allows you to speak both to your audience in the room and the people online. Consider using several screens if you need to in order to make sure that you are seen and that all participants can see the screen.

Ensure engagement through individual presence

During the session be sure you are all present to ensure engagement from everyone. Be on video – personally – all of you. Sitting alone watching some people as close-ups and others as a pixelated group does not support a good meeting. Everyone needs to ensure a proper individual setup and it's your job as facilitator to help and remind them.

When you check in, do it in such a way that everyone is included and gets to speak. Do a round where everyone checks in if you are few in number. If there are more than 6–8 people then organise into smaller breakout rooms, preferably with a mix of people connecting to the meeting virtually and people physically present in the meeting room. Take care not to exclude either the 'physical' or 'online' participants.

Connect people in different ways

We recommend connecting people in different ways instead of going for the 'physical together and virtual together option'. You can get the participants who are physically together to discuss something, but you should also mix and match across the physical room and the virtual space.

Visualise so everyone can follow

We prefer to document everything online so that everyone can see it. That means you need your own device as the facilitator. If you chose to go for old-school documentation make sure that it is visible and readable on screen. It could be using a flip. Be aware that all can contribute – not only the people able to grasp the pen – e.g. you as the facilitator can write inputs on the flip.

> *Top tip: Use walk and talk if you want to have break-out conversations between physical and online participants, if you need some fresh air, to inject some energy or if the sound is an issue.*

After the hybrid meeting

As with any meeting you should ensure that you get feedback, and follow up with participants. As hybrid meetings can be difficult to handle, we strongly recommend that you add time for feedback – both if this is a one-off session or recurring. This allows you to get even more inputs on how to ensure high-quality interactions while still providing the flexibility that hybrid meetings offer.

Case: Combined leadership seminar for 25 executives in four locations

Purpose	To develop the leadership team and the business at the same time by discussion and sharing learnings from three months of coronavirus lockdown, and agree on a leadership focus for the organisation going forward.
	Take next step in a leadership development programme and ignite learning groups and personal development sprints.
Success criteria	• Share and produce five key leadership learnings post-coronavirus.
	• Agree on personal development focus for the next three months.
	• Meetings booked for learning group dialogues.
	• Participants leave energised and inspired both on content AND in the form of the meeting, inspiring them to similar things in their own leadership team.
Participants	• 25 top executives covering all business units and support function of a business with 3,000+ employees across multiple locations, countries and brands.

(Continued)

Case: Combined leadership seminar for 25 executives in four locations

Platform	• 4 physical locations across the country hosting 4–8 participants in each.
	• Teams and video conferencing equipment.
	• Phone for walk and talk.
	• Shared files (Excel and PowerPoint for tasks).
Process	• A mix of shared online inspirational talks, table discussions in the 4 physical rooms supported by templates and virtual learning group dialogues across locations including a 'virtual walk and talk'.
Partners	• CEO setting the strategic direction
	• Facilitators in each room
	• External inspirational talks on leadership and behavioural design sprint
The solution	The organisation had launched an ambitious leadership development program for the executive team just before the coronavirus pandemic locked down the countries in which the organisation had operations. After the first two months of firefighting the CEO realised that it was more important than ever to keep the leadership development process alive. The solution was to re-launch the programme by spending a day together focusing purely on leadership despite the big business challenges at hand. Due to restrictions we designed a workshop that was a combination of different ways of interacting – both to create variation and, equally, to inspire the executive team to use some of the forms in their own way of working.

Case: Combined leadership seminar for 25 executives in four locations

The first part of the day was all about getting together again with the focus on strategy and leadership and not operational KPI. The CEO gave his strategic perspective which he had shared with the board the day before heading into a Q&A session, where smaller groups at each location had to produce questions to increase the quality and edge of the questions.

After a break, the physical groups talked about their leadership actions and learning during the coronavirus period. The instruction was given through teams, and each physical location had to document their takeaways in a shared PowerPoint file with a template for each group. Each group shared virtually at the end their learnings and the consultant shared the learnings from other organisations and how to rebound from crisis with learnings from the financial crisis.

After lunch the focus changed towards the individual leader that, through a strict 'sprint' process, developed his/her own development activities targeted at changing personal leadership behaviour in the months to come. To support this we launched learning groups with people from the different physical locations and connected them through Team meetings in groups of four and sent them out on a virtual walk and talk. After sharing and refining the development activities the groups came back to their respective physical rooms and booked different development activities through Excel and Outlook (learning group meetings, Hogan assessment dialogues, coaching sessions). The session was wrapped up with an energetic closing session uniting the four locations as ONE executive team.

25

Virtual Workshops

This deep dive is about how to facilitate highly effective virtual workshops. When we run a virtual workshop, we're bringing people together to do work. This is a space where we want them to be mentally switched on and engaged most of the time. We might be working on a project, consulting with the participants, testing some assumptions, or asking for the input of our participants and co-creating with them.

Virtual workshops can be highly effective if they are executed correctly. Using virtual formats gives you the option of running more frequent but shorter sessions, because you don't have to worry about travelling to a venue or altering your setup to allow for different locations. Using virtual workshops also allows you to have time between sessions where the participants can complete homework or practical training. This all gives you greater flexibility.

Virtual workshops are usually between an hour and a half and three to four hours long. Five hours is the absolute maximum length we recommend for a virtual workshop.

In this chapter, we'll talk about facilitating workshops for between 4 and 20 participants. If you have more participants than this, move to Chapter 27 about virtual large-scale events. The key thing to remember with workshops is that they need to be highly engaging and interactive. You need to remove all the barriers to participation to encourage everyone in the workshop to share their input.

Workshops aren't about you delivering information. They are predominantly about encouraging input and getting everyone to cooperate.

Benefits of virtual workshops

In some respects, virtual workshops might not sound that different to physical workshops, but they offer some important benefits. One of the main ones is that you're able to engage people across the whole world.

Throughout the process you can bring in experts, testers, users or consumers to provide their feedback and input and to help move things along. These people can just join for a small part of the workshop, maybe 20 minutes, and then leave. This is one of the huge benefits of the virtual space, because you don't need to physically get people to travel. You can introduce expert knowledge or valuable insights very quickly and easily.

> *Top tip: Don't be afraid of inviting people to join just one small part of your workshop to provide their input. Get experts, customers or other users to come in, co-create with you and then leave once their part has finished.*

In our experience, virtual workshops can often be more efficient than physical workshops, provided they are planned properly. This is particularly the case when it comes to decision-making since it is much harder to 'read the room', so you need to be clear on the decision criteria and how you will run the decision process.

Before a virtual workshop

When you're planning a virtual workshop the most important thing to be aware of is that it can go in different directions on the day. As the facilitator, your job is to make sure everyone participates actively and that you move towards the purpose of your workshop.

Because virtual workshops can take a different direction to the one you expected, the key is to over plan. Work through every point on the Design Star and be thorough.

> *Top tip: It is hard to improvise in a virtual meeting, so if you foresee the need, then plan for 2–3 scenarios in advance with different templates and exercises.*

Selecting the right platform

Be especially aware when you consider what platform to use, to select one that will allow you to create the most interaction during the workshop, and which platform will be easiest for the participants to use. These elements go hand in hand.

Another really important aspect to planning a virtual workshop is that you need to plan how you will capture the outputs. Think about what sort of platform can accommodate this depending on the purpose of the workshop: are you working on a project, consulting or co-creating?

Ensure participants knows how to use the platform

When you're planning to introduce a new tool, such as a new whiteboard tool, create a prep session that you can go through with your participants – to introduce the tool and make sure that they all know how to use it effectively right from the start. You should arrange this as a separate session ahead of the workshop if possible, or include it near the very start of your workshop if you have to wait until the day. If your participants have high-tech skills already it might be enough with a small introduction video of the platform, a log-in and a preparation task using the platform.

Looking at the process be aware that even though we tend to be more efficient in virtual sessions, people are often too optimistic about what can be achieved in the timeframe they have for their workshop.

> *Top tip: Plan 10–20% additional time into your workshop, compared to what you think you need. You have to allow for the fact that people might need a bit more time getting used to the tools, understanding the exercises or recapping. Don't make a tight plan for your workshop and don't be surprised if you have to deviate from your plan during the session. Most people will be okay with you ending ahead of schedule too!*

Set expectations prior to the session

Before you go into the workshop, make the participants aware that they will be expected to contribute during this session. Tell them that this isn't a passive meeting. You can use this opportunity to explain the reasons for the workshop, why it's important, and encourage them to bring fresh knowledge or creativity to the table. Also tell your participants what you will use their input for and how you will encourage them to provide their input during the workshop. It's important to communicate this beforehand to give them time to prepare.

Although you should allow space in your session for deviation, you should still make sure that you plan your virtual processes thoroughly.

> *Top tip: Set up templates ready for the participants to fill in, so that they aren't starting with a blank sheet every time you send them into an exercise. Use a PowerPoint slide, whiteboard or whatever platform is most appropriate to provide a structured way to gather input.*

Create a template or framework that makes it easy to contribute

The more of a framework you can provide for your participants, the easier it will be for them to understand the problem and categorise their thoughts and input; and the more efficient the process will be. This is also really important to help you document the inputs after the workshop. You'll find some examples of virtual process templates to help you with this aspect of planning a workshop in our online resources. www.implement.dk/vf#methods

> *Top tip: If you are planning a simple kind of workshop that you are going to run many times, such as a team start or project start workshop, think about how you can put a bit more effort into it to make the setup really cool.*

Make sure to plan who is in charge of documenting what is agreed. As facilitator this frees you up to focus on the process. It also provides a really useful reference that you can use to recap and share what you've accomplished with the participants.

During a virtual workshop

It's important that you get off on the right foot when you start a virtual workshop. We would recommend that you begin by framing the session, explaining the purpose and why you are gathered here, as well as being clear about what the output from the workshop will be used for. It's your job to give everyone the context and the story behind the workshop. You're connecting the dots.

Make sure that everyone knows what has already been decided so that you don't waste time on something that isn't relevant to the purpose of this workshop.

It's also important to set out, at the start of the session, how you expect your participants to engage and to make each one of them feel like their input is valuable. It's your responsibility to make them feel as though they belong in the workshop and clearly share the reason why they are there.

> *Top tip: Engage the participants from the start by conducting an Opener such as 'Around the Table'. Introduce each participant, explain why they have been invited to the session and set out any special roles they may have in the process.*

As the facilitator it's also your job to regulate the energy of your participants throughout the session. You need to make sure they are in a good place where they feel that they can contribute throughout the workshop. Remember to check in regularly with people, ask how their energy levels are and whether they feel able to contribute. Don't be afraid of introducing breaks and energisers throughout the session to regulate their state of mind and energy levels.

Ask if they feel as though they have the right input to enable them to continue. In a workshop you need to check in with your participants about their level of knowledge, their state of mind and their energy levels.

Remember to create clarity throughout your workshop. Give clear instructions to ensure that people know what to do in exercises, whiteboards or virtual collaboration platforms. This is especially important if you're using breakout rooms, because if the people in the workshop know each other they might want to discuss other things.

> *Top tip: Get your participants in breakout rooms to document what they talk about. It's a good way to ensure that people are working on the right thing because no one wants to have a blank document to present to the rest of the group.*

When people are using virtual tools to capture their inputs, such as a whiteboard or slides, it's really important that they write in full sentences. Everything they capture should make sense to someone who reads it afterwards and who wasn't in the session. Tell them that you'll be sending these inputs to someone else and that they need to be able to make sense of it. Remind them of this each time they go into an exercise.

You can use the feedback tools we provided in Chapter 20 during your workshop if you are using the session to test a product or a solution.

It's very important that you stay on top of the process during your workshop. Workshops involve a lot of talking and discussion, which can take the session in different ways. As the facilitator, it's your job to ensure that these discussions don't get out of hand. Use timeboxing for your exercises and make sure that you frame exactly what should be talked about. Also engage with participants if you need to change the plan. You can ask if they find it important to use extra time on one thing, to skip another, or postpone the decision.

It's your job to ensure you reach the purpose. This might include being strict about time and telling the participants very clearly how long they have for each discussion. As the facilitator, be prepared to close people down or redirect them to get them back on track.

When you reach the end of the session, always connect the dots. Make sense of what has just happened by telling your participants what will happen next. Show them that this workshop wasn't about pseudo-involvement but that there will be real-life applications from what they have worked on. You need to show them where this fits into the big picture and where you are in the process at that moment.

> *Top tip: Be ready to zoom out and give them the full journey if that's required. Sometimes we can get lost in the process when we're in a workshop focusing on specific exercises. As the facilitator, you need to be able to give people the big picture and then zoom them back in to show them where you are right now.*

After a virtual workshop

It's always recommendable to evaluate your workshops and gather feedback, like we discussed in Chapter 20. Use tools like polls or surveys to collect data-driven insights. It's also important that you follow up with your participants.

In the follow-up we suggest showing your participants how you used their inputs. You could create a report, send them a snapshot of what was discussed, a picture from the meeting, or simply the highlights of the plans going forward.

> *Top tip: Always save a little something that you can share as a post-workshop update with the group. This will help to motivate them and reinforce that they're part of a meaningful project with a purpose. It will give them something to be proud of and this can help create change. Your participants can become ambassadors. Make sure they know that the project is still alive, even if they're not part of any ongoing meetings.*

When you use digital collaboration tools, some of the work after a workshop is made a lot easier for you because the documentation is ready immediately. You don't need to sift through Post-it notes to make sense of what people discussed and created.

If you record your workshop, you can use this to evaluate your own performance. Watch the workshop back and use that to evaluate how you come across, to help you learn and develop as a facilitator.

Things to be aware of

In virtual workshops, it can be easier to lose sight of the overview than it is in a physical setting. You often only tackle one topic during a virtual workshop because you can't run a session like this for more than a few hours. Because you don't have physical reminders (such as flip charts around the walls) of what has happened before, it can be harder to refer back to things and see where you are in the process. This is why it's important that the facilitator is always ready to share the journey with people and visualise the process and the work.

You also need to be aware that you can sometimes miss out on relationship building during a virtual workshop. In a physical session, people would make small talk during a coffee break and so on, and you can lose this in the virtual world if you don't facilitate time for that social connection. If you will be running a series of workshops with the same group of participants, such as over the course of a project, you may want to consider running the first session as a physical one to encourage that relationship building, if you have the luxury of doing so.

How to run a virtual whiteboard jam session

Running a whiteboard jam session virtually can be more structured and tangible than a physical one. One thing we often hear is that people miss the kinaesthetic feeling associated with writing by hand on a whiteboard. Sometimes we think of standing with a pen and physically writing on a board as being creative. But there's no reason why you can't allow people to physically write during a virtual whiteboard jam session.

Allow time in your workshop for people to grab a pen and paper and actually write. Give them five minutes to do a hand drawing on the piece of paper they have in front of them. Then ask everyone to take a photo of their page and share it with the group by uploading it to the virtual whiteboard.

Often people will draw more quickly with a pen and paper and it gives them a chance to just follow their thoughts. The key message is: don't be afraid of stepping into the physical environment and then finding a way to bring it back to the virtual.

Although there are tools available that allow people to write directly onto a digital whiteboard, they can be quite expensive and not everyone will have access to them. Look for simple solutions, like using a pen and paper and then taking a photo and uploading it. If you choose a high-tech solution, master it as the facilitator and allow time for your participants to learn how to use it too.

If you're in a hybrid workshop, like we discussed in the previous chapter, where you have some people sitting in a room together and others joining virtually from elsewhere in the world, we strongly recommend that you limit what you do on a physical whiteboard with the participants who are in the room with you. It's far better to ask everyone to complete exercises virtually using a digital whiteboard so that everyone feels as though they are involved and able to contribute.

Case: Virtual Design Sprint on HR processes

Purpose	The purpose of these workshops was to develop prototypes for optimising the recruitment process. The process was part of initiative in developing a new HR system.
Success criteria	• Develop six specific prototypes for optimising the recruitment process developed with input from 'customers' using the HR system. • Get feedback from the leadership team.
Participants	Approx. 20 participants from HR representing various regions/locations around the world, business representatives and top HR management.
Environment / platform	Zoom as communication platform. Miro as whiteboard tool for prototype development.
Process	A structured process using design thinking techniques for problem definition, idea generation and prototyping. The process takes one week (five days) and each session is five hours long.
Partners	2 facilitators (one facilitator, one technical assistant 3 advisors with expert knowledge 6 costumers to get intro from 6 managers to review prototypes

The solution

Participants were invited to a test session where they were introduced to the software used during the week (Zoom + Miro). In addition the purpose was to get acquainted with the special way of working in the Design Sprint method.

The process included five workshops, one for each day in the week:

Day 1: Focus on defining a clear framing of the optimisation of the HR processes using 'How might we question.' Customers and important stakeholders are interviewed and share their frustration and wishes. Inputs are documented as notes into the predefined whiteboard in Miro on sticky notes. At the end of the day, they are compiled into a single good question.

Day 2: Focus on idea generation producing as many ideas as possible by working according to a specific idea generation method called 'crazy 8'. Here, participants draw eight ideas on a piece of physical paper, and upload to the common whiteboard in Miro.

The ideas are boiled together into three solutions and participants vote on which ones to continue working with.

Day 3: Focus on developing the chosen solution and describing a prototype on a visual storyboard in the whiteboard. Screen dumps are inserted and described in the visual mock-up.

Day 4: The prototype is presented to the customers; feedback is provided and the prototype improved according to this.

Day 5: The overall solution is presented to the management team and the next step is agreed on.

Special takeaways from this case

- It takes a lot of planning to run a virtual Design Sprint.
- Dedicate two facilitators to handle the process and technical issues if necessary.
- Make it very visual by combining a virtual whiteboard and physical note taking.
- Timebox everything and use timer to visualise it to force the participants to take decisions and move forward.

26

Virtual Training

Virtual training are designed to simulate the traditional classroom or learning experience. This isn't a completely new world; many virtual training programs have been running for years. What we need to do is build upon what we already know about learning and learning principles. Don't forget everything you know about engagement, involvement and learning processes.

One of the main reasons why you conduct virtual training is because you have participants who need to acquire a new skill or knowledge in a specific area. The aim of the training is to get the participants to change their behaviour; you want them to do something differently when they go back to their job. In this instance, it's important that they have a facilitator and instructor who can guide them through the process and give them feedback.

The other main reason why you conduct virtual training is to reach a global audience when it's not possible to meet physically. Virtual training in either instance can enable you to have more frequent touchpoints and ensure behaviour change happens among your participants.

When you are delivering virtual training, your role as a facilitator changes. You become the trainer and that means you'll need to provide both more content and handle other processes. It also allows you to put your opinion out there and give feedback.

There are different types of virtual training methods, and virtual training can be conducted synchronously and asynchronously. Synchronous training is instructor-led training, where social learning plays a big part. Asynchronous training is non-instructor led, with the student going through content at their own pace and receiving less support.

For the purposes of this deep dive, we're going to focus on virtual instructor-led training. This means that the learners need to work together to achieve a common goal, exchange views, clarify the meanings of a concept or solve problems together. As the trainer, it's your job to create opportunities for cooperation in skills development. The emphasis is on interaction with your participants. You're getting the participants to understand the topic, discuss it and develop it precisely by exploring the differences between the participants' levels of knowledge.

In terms of facilitating virtual instructor-led training, you need to ensure your session focuses on engaging with the participants, and that you strike the right balance between providing input and practical exercises.

Before we dive into the before, during and after of virtual training sessions, it's important that you understand a little about neuroplasticity and learning. The mind can be changed. What we know about fostering neuroplasticity is that you can change your brain by creating new connections within it. This requires electricity – basically the mind needs to be fired up.[1] As a trainer, this is what your job is all about if you want to foster learning. You need to create exercises that present the opportunity for participants to develop new electrical connections in their brains. When the neurons fire together enough times, they wire

[1] The developing brain, Shatz, CJ, *Scientific American* 1992 Sep; 267(3):60-7.

together. This is what creates learning. You provide the framework and your participants need to train and do it, in order to actually learn it. Further on in the chapter you'll find a model for fostering neuroplasticity and learning, where we talk about readiness, construction and consolidation. These are the main factors that create electricity, which in turn encourages the neurons to fire together and wire together.

Our approach to learning

We don't believe in the old-school concept of learning, whereby you told people to do something and that resulted in behaviour change. We believe learning is about creating connections in the brain, and this is why people need to be active in their own learning process to develop behaviour change.

It's not enough for them to see someone else share a slide, hear very clever words or to see someone else demonstrating the desired skill. People need to hear themselves saying it. They need to work on the activities themselves. What's most important is that they try out what they learn. They need to experiment and test their assumptions. They might even want to learn socially, with the other people that they are in the session with.

We also know that learning can't happen in isolation. It needs to be contextual. When I learn from a situation, it's important that it's relevant to me in order for me to learn it. It's important that the activities are a part of my everyday work. As the facilitator and trainer, that means you can't just take one process and replicate it for lots of different groups. You always need to think about how you can design your process to make the training meaningful for your participants and adjust it accordingly.

Before a virtual training session

Of course you start with your Design Star. What's really important here is that you are clear on the instructional goals and the performance objective, and that you describe people's roles within the design process. You need to identify the overarching goals for the session, know what you are trying to achieve and know what information should be shared or what skills need to be learned to achieve your purpose.

> *Top tip: Put most of your time into exercises that train your participants in the skills needed, rather than just focusing on the knowledge.*

This is an example of how you can translate the purpose of your training into knowledge and a skill.

Purpose: For managers to have better one-on-one conversations with their employees so they feel motivated and inspired to develop within the company.
Knowledge: Understand what motivates people.
Skill: How to facilitate a great feedback dialogue.

In training sessions be aware of the number of participants. Is the purpose or topic suited for a large group or will it work better with a small group? You might have a set group of participants already and, if this is the case, you should figure out who they are, and what they already know.

> *Top tip: The more feedback you need to provide and the more complex the training is, the smaller the session should be.*

When it comes to designing your process for the training, it's about making sure that you have an appropriate learning journey. Is it a one-off training of two hours or a full programme with several interactions, tasks in between, reflection groups and readings? One of the benefits of the virtual format is that it's much easier to get people together for short periods of time, and many people actually prefer doing activities, having a break and then returning to learning. Use this to your advantage. Figure 26.1 illustrates how a learning journey might look.

> *Top tip: Break longer training sessions into multiple smaller sessions to ensure your participants don't lose focus.*

When you are designing your process you need to allow for frequent interactions between the participants and the trainer. The general rule of thumb is that every five minutes you should include some kind of involvement. Ask for their opinions, get their reflections on what they've just learned. Find out how much they agree with what you're saying and how they relate to it. These micro-involvements and check-ins with the group are essential.

When you look at the platform, select one that creates room for interaction and training to support the learning journey of the individual. Think about how you want participants to interact. Will you be able to use one platform, or will you need several to facilitate your training?

> *Top tip: Build a quiz (or multiple quizzes) into your session. Quizzes provide an opportunity for participants to test their knowledge. It's a good way for them to check in with their learning. You can use them to break up the session and provide a distinction between different learning points. As a trainer, it's also a good way to get feedback on what knowledge people have retained.*

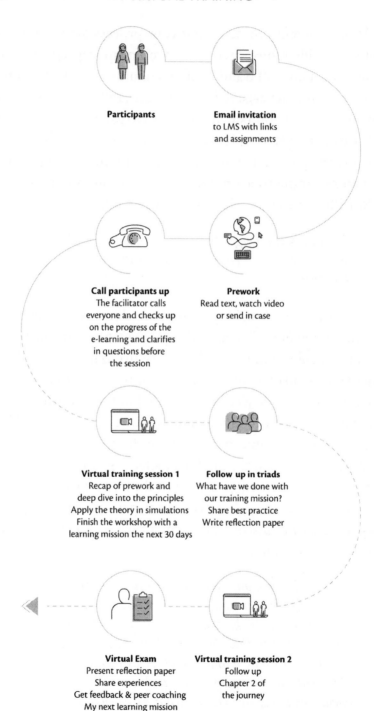

Participants

Email invitation
to LMS with links
and assignments

Call participants up
The facilitator calls
everyone and checks up
on the progress of the
e-learning and clarifies
in questions before
the session

Prework
Read text, watch video
or send in case

Virtual training session 1
Recap of prework and
deep dive into the principles
Apply the theory in simulations
Finish the workshop with a
learning mission the next 30 days

Follow up in triads
What have we done with
our training mission?
Share best practice
Write reflection paper

Virtual Exam
Present reflection paper
Share experiences
Get feedback & peer coaching
My next learning mission

Virtual training session 2
Follow up
Chapter 2 of
the journey

Figure 26.1   A sample learning journey

As a general rule in training, we recommend having a check-in on learnings every 20 to 30 minutes during your session – through a quiz, dialogues, reflections, tasks etc.

Breakout rooms are an important element to design into your virtual training session because they provide the opportunity for social learning reflection. You're also creating a space that feels psychologically safe for the participants. Breakouts are a great opportunity for peer feedback, and they allow your participants to test their assumptions and learn with each other.

Set your participants' expectations before the session

Prior to the training we recommend that you make it relevant to the participants. You need to tell your participants very clearly what's in it for them. Why is this training relevant? We're talking about readiness for the training. Readiness means making sure that everyone's minds are in a good place, that they aren't going to overload when they come into the session and that they are also ready to open up for learning. To help with this, it can be a good idea to tell your participants what they will be learning about. You might show them the learning principles, or the journey, so that they start building a mental picture of how the training will work.

One option is to set preparation tasks for your participants. This could be to encourage people to think about what they need to learn prior to the session. Another example could be to ask each participant to interview two prior participants for feedback on their facilitation skills if you were to train facilitation. Or you could send out a preread or a test. If you are going to take this approach, tell your participants that they not only need to block out time for the session itself, but also to complete the work that you will set each day.

This also has to do with creating prior knowledge for the session – if you can front-load some knowledge where people read or watch an e-learning in advance you can spend more time actually training during the session.

Top tip: Find a creative way to share your pre-exposure content. You could write an article, shoot a movie trailer for the session, create a screen recording, send an email, share a slide. This can be anything that provides your participants with an overview of the session. The idea is to paint the big picture and make them curious to learn more.

Create psychological safety

In a learning situation psychological safety is key to a good learning environment. If people don't feel safe they are less likely to share what they find difficult or be honest in dialogues. It's your job as facilitator and trainer to create this. First, you should have people using the webcams. Second, don't underestimate the importance of social openers and energisers during the session. Finally, you can use breakout rooms to make smaller groups with room for more vulnerability. If you stick with the same groups and they get to know each other these smaller groups will most likely build trust quite fast.

During a virtual training session

During the session is when you want to construct new knowledge. We focus on coherent construction, and that means all the participants need to be very active themselves during the session. We believe that you, as a trainer, can't ensure learning. You can provide the framework and new content, but it's the participants who should work with this to learn in practice. Everything else we've talked about here is still true, but what is especially important in a virtual training environment is chunking.

Suggestions for chunking up your content

- Break it down into bite-sized pieces.
- You shouldn't have a lot of slides or slides with a lot of text on them; less is more.
- Introduce animation.
- Highlight the key message in each of your slides.
- Give people time to apply the key message before continuing with new content. You want to avoid cognitive overload by giving them too much information too quickly.

Training engagement

Training engagement is what we've discussed previously in relation to micro-involvements. That means you should utilise polls, quizzes and other interactive formats every five minutes – all of the elements we discussed when it comes to planning your training session.

Look at the tips and tricks in Chapter 15 to create engagement and make sure that you, as a trainer, support it during the session.

> *Top tip: Create excitement about what is going to happen in your session. Tell the participants what they will be able to do with their new superpowers. Share a good story about what other people have done afterwards, what they have used their skills for and what they have achieved.*

Give people time

Another thing that's important in terms of engagement is to give the participants time throughout the session to talk about what the training means to them. In doing this, you're creating time for transferring their knowledge and simultaneously improving engagement. All the way through the session, make sure you're giving people the opportunity to relate to what they're learning, to give them time to test it and to see how this can be applied in their own lives.

Use multisensory instruction

This is about trying to activate as much of the brain as possible. What we know is that people need to learn from different pathways and you should include as many as possible in your session. That means being very visual in your slides, using colours and getting people to write down things themselves. Try to activate the auditory cortex. This is what you hear, so make sure people have the chance to hear themselves talk, and when you are giving instructions vary your tone of voice so that it goes up and down in pitch. The hardest area to activate in the virtual space is the motor cortex. This is all about activating your physical body. To do this virtually, consider whether you want to get people to write notes by hand, using a pen and paper. Maybe you want people to use their bodies in front of the webcam, so they can gesture; and think about how you can use breaks and energisers to make people move their bodies.

Feedback

The final element to consider during your session is feedback. It's important that you close down any incorrect learnings and get feedback from the participants and check in with what they've learned. This is also about allowing people to check in with themselves.

Top tip: You can give feedback as the facilitator, you can encourage peer-to-peer feedback, you can also have a checklist, a video or maybe some guiding questions. Quizzes are a great way to test understanding.

Breakout rooms can be a good way to enable peer-to-peer feedback. People can break up into small groups, do some work and then come back together in plenary. In this way, you encourage peer feedback through discussion in the breakouts. You could also get your participants to use the comment feature to add their thoughts to the group work and provide feedback in this way.

After a virtual training session

After the training session has ended you will immediately start fighting the forgetting curve. People usually forget quite quickly if they aren't given the opportunity to retrieve or revisit the content. When you're designing your session, split your content up so that people not only visit this content during the session, but that they also recap what they have learned after the session is over. You want them to revisit the content the next day, three days later and maybe even a week later too. You could consider sending out emails in a systematic order to remind them.

Top tip: Give people the opportunity to revisit what they have learned in their own minds. Also make sure that they have the opportunity to talk to each other and share what they have learned. This reinforces the learning from their training session.

Spacing the learning is one of the most important things to consider in terms of the virtual classroom. It might feel a little counter-intuitive, but we know that for learning to happen you need to step away from it. It's really important to give people this opportunity, because taking a step back from the process of learning puts them in a state where learning is really effective. Often when you come back to it, you find that what you have learned has become embedded in your long-term memory.

> *Top tip: Consider having a lot of sessions and making these small bite-sized sessions to give people the space and opportunity to leave and come back to their learning. You can also add tasks to be completed in between the sessions to ensure continued focus.*

Don't be afraid of repeating yourself or letting your participants repeat themselves, because this also helps to reinforce their learning.

What has the greatest effect on the transfer of training?

When you look at how we learn, you discover that 20% of this effect comes from the training session itself; 35% of the effect comes from personal factors, such as how motivated your participants are and how much they believe in themselves; and 45% of the effect comes from the application and the context, which is when they are out there in the real world, using what they learned.[2] When you're delivering virtual training, you need

---

[2] *Voksenpædagogik*, Bjarne Wahlgren, Saxo 2018.

to think about whether your participants have everything they need after the session and whether they are supported to use what they have learned.

> *Top tip: The learning journey doesn't end after the session. We recommend including 'after tasks' in the design and checking in with your participants after the session to find out if they are applying what they learned. Make sure you provide them with the content they need to use in their own environment. That might be providing support in their job, setting up communities, or simply for you to provide feedback and help where it's needed.*

It's important to understand that you won't tap into this 45% of the effect from application if you don't run a good training session that is high quality, encourages motivation and gives people personal belief. A good training session is a prerequisite for creating that impact. However, the training session itself isn't what creates the direct effect; it is an enabler to allow the rest to follow.

Case: Virtual sales training

Virtual Selling is here to stay, and post Covid-19, many commercial organisations will have transformed into a more Virtual Sales model. This case describes an end-to-end Virtual Capability Development Programme to help commercial organisations successfully drive their virtual sales transformation.

During the spring of 2020 we up-skilled over 500 commercial managers globally on effective virtual customer interactions.

(Continued)

Purpose	During Covid-19 all meetings became virtual – sales people working with customers had to move into a virtual universe to stay relevant. Many sales people globally were not equipped to run an effective customer meeting online. As a salesperson you normally rely on physical materials and a presentation as back drop, but personal relations and charisma are key. In the virtual space you need to design your content to carry the weight. The purpose of the training sessions is to address barriers, and learn how to prepare, execute and follow up on virtual customer meetings. The client in this case – a global B2B biotech organisation– recognised that their commercial people needed support to build their comfort level in virtual interactions. Their competencies, their skills – their toolset.
Success criteria	• Sales people feel confident, competent and have the skillset to interact with customers online. • To frame the mindset of the participants during the virtual sales meeting: You are responsible for the outcome – steering the meeting, addressing the issue, the customer's experience of the meeting.
Participants	Commercially focused people in the organisation: marketing people, business development functions, salespeople.
Platform	Communication platform with an option for sharing slides and doing breakout rooms, e.g. Teams or Zoom.
Process	We practice what we preach – selling the training is done by the principles that we teach! Pre-read for participants 2½-hour training session Follow-up tasks
Partners	1 facilitator for 10 or 20 participants

The solution

Training sales virtually

The virtual sales training is all about getting into the mindset of what virtual selling requires, knowing the Virtual Sales model and trying it out in practice to learn how to use it with customers. This includes:

- Knowing the process of a successful virtual sales meeting.
- Diving into the preparation phase: preparation for your virtual sales meeting is crucial – when you have fewer opportunities to freestyle in the virtual space you need to prepare well.
- Training the process in practice with lots of smaller exercises and micro-interactions to demonstrate how it can be done and start learning it right away.
- During the training there is a specific focus on how you build trust in a virtual space.

Commercial activities and selling products or services is all about trust. You need to build trust to make sure that you have a customer dialogue where you can share difficult things/pains. In the virtual space we don't have the same tool to create trust as we have in the physical world.

A key point during the training is to deliberately dedicate time to build trust. Don't just go straight to your products or services. One way to do this is to invite people to join in five minutes before the formal meeting where the host facilitates the conversation with questions such as: How are you? Where are you calling in from? How is your energy level? Build on whatever you hear. Informal talk is not only ok, it's important.

During the session also allow for elements that increase trust.

27

Virtual Large-Scale Events

Facilitating virtual large-scale events is a discipline that requires strong skills within virtual facilitation. We define a large-scale event as one where you gather more than 50 people together at the same time. The key thing to understand is that these take a lot of preparation – more than the normal amount – to make sure that you get maximum impact out of them and that your participants leave with the right feeling when they finish, and with the right produced input from you.

Before a virtual large-scale event

One of the most important things to decide in the planning phase is what type of format you are going to run. Will it be mainly one-way webinars, a town hall, presentations, a selling-in exercise, or a workshop where you co-create? Deciding which of these formats you'll use is crucial because each one sets off a different planning phase. Regardless of what format your event will take, you still always start with the purpose at the centre of

Examples of virtual large-scale events

- A day-long summit on a specific topic, such as if you're bringing 100 managers together for the launch of a new system.
- A multi-day event, for example where you roll out a commercial or strategic solution across multiple countries and locations.
- A digital learning journey.
- Stacked micro-sessions.
- A virtual open space.
- A virtual hackathon.
- Multiple connected physical sessions, for instance where you have several people together in various meeting rooms spread across the world, who, combined in the virtual space.

the Design Star. What is the purpose of this large-scale event? Is it to inform, is it to produce something, or is it to sense-make with a big audience?

Sometimes you won't have control over how many participants there are; that might be predetermined. In other circumstances you may have some influence over that. As a general rule, the more people you are getting together for a virtual large-scale event, the more time you need to spend in the design and planning of your session. This is because you need to make sure that you cater properly for the many people who will be spending their time joining your session, as well as that you use the right platforms and have the right partners in your team. You can't improvise in the moment or deviate from your plan.

When you shouldn't run virtual large-scale sessions

There are situations when it's not appropriate to run virtual large-scale sessions, such as:

- To create trust: If there's a lack of trust within a large group or you have some tension or conflict that needs mediation, it's better to consider meeting people in smaller groups with a leader. These kinds of issues are usually best dealt with in smaller groups.
- You/your participants lack the basic technology: Make sure you know what technology your participants have access to. If only half of the firm will be able to attend, or if they don't have the right technology to participate in full, your event can backfire.
- You're an inexperienced virtual facilitator: If you aren't a very experienced virtual facilitator, get help with running a large-scale session or don't do it, otherwise this can look unprofessional and will also backfire.

Top tip: Play it safe. Choose the lowest denominator in terms of platform experience. You want to avoid people stretching their capabilities too much. Always play it safe and get more help with facilitating the session in the form of a co-facilitator and/or tech assistant. Make sure you test the platform and do dry runs. This will all help you to feel confident that it will run smoothly and professionally on the day.

One of the most important things you can do once you've designed and planned the session is a dry run. This gives you a chance to see how everything works on the tech side. You can check your slides and videos, if you have them. For example, we've seen people insist on using videos in their slides during their large-scale session, but the problem is that PowerPoint and videos aren't a good mix. The intention may be good, but it creates a lot of difficulty for the people watching and stress among the facilitators who are trying to make it work.

Again, our advice with virtual large-scale events is that it's always better to take one step down in terms of complexity, in terms of the platform you use, and in terms of your own role and engagement in it. Over time, as you gain more experience, you can increase the complexity of your future virtual large-scale events.

You need to be very clear in virtual large-scale events and firmly set out your corner flags. Keep any presentations firmly on topic. If you're running a section where you want the participants to provide input, you need to be even more firm about what's up for discussion before you get started with a lot of people. Clearly align expectations of what the session is about before you actually run it.

Make sure you also plan for some engagement with your participants. Although we recommend taking a step down in terms of complexity, you shouldn't forget about engagement with your participants completely. Challenge yourself to make this more than just a one-way video production – think about how you can engage with people, and plan the form that engagement will take.

Top tip: Remember engagement doesn't need to be big. It might be checking in on the chat, running a small breakout element, or getting people to wave to the camera. It just needs to be anything that makes your participants connect a little bit. Plan this engagement in the before phase so that your participants don't end up feeling like they've just leaned back and watched a movie.

If the virtual large-scale event you're running is more like a workshop, then think carefully about how much input you want from participants and what format you want that input in. If you don't think about this before, then during the session you could have 50, 100 or even 150 people all producing input and you won't be able to manage it. Do you want input on one idea or five ideas, for instance? What format will their input be in? If 200 people start writing in the chat, it's almost impossible to condense that afterwards. If you think carefully about these elements in the before phase, it will make it easier for you to process it afterwards.

You'll also need to spend a bit more time on the partners point of the Design Star than you would on some of the other virtual meeting formats we've discussed. With virtual large-scale events you normally have more partners in terms of producing the session with a host, a co-facilitator and a technical assistant as well as people providing subject matter expertise or leaders joining to contribute at some point.

It takes time to align the format with the time spent, the PowerPoints and all these other elements. These things all need to be clarified so that your session comes across as smooth and professional.

You also need to dedicate a lot of time to your tech setup. As we discussed in Chapter 4, you'll want at least three screens for your tech setup (You need to be apple to display: A screen for shared content with participants, showing next slide, displaying videos, the video conference, and miscellaneous applications), you'll want good lighting and you should have the option of standing up or moving around. If it's possible, have a camera operator who can move around with you, because this can bring a bit more life into your session than if you just have a steady, fixed camera.

> *Top tip: Put tape on the floor before you start so you know exactly where the camera is pointing and where you need to stand to be properly framed.*

You should also agree on some areas that are off limits, where one of your helpers can stand out of shot and give you signs about where you're at, and so on. It's vital to do a dry run of the playbook, using the roles and agreements that you put in place. Also make sure you test the tech solution to ensure it's not too complex either for you or your participants to use.

You also want to think about how you can get your participants excited about attending your event. You could send out a teaser video in advance, for instance, to create attention and hype around the session.

How-to design: Virtual large scale

Step 1: What is the purpose of your virtual large-scale workshop/event?

- Strategic processes, development, testing, cultural processes, value and principle definition or validation, kick-off for major projects or transformations, technical events.

Step 2: What output do you expect?

- Increased engagement, increased ownership, co-created results.
- Just double-checking if a virtual format really is the right fit.

Step 3: How long will it take?

- What is the duration of overall engagement? You might want to check if you need to split up the workshop into several sessions. You can do this by taking breaks throughout the day or scheduling it as a journey across several weeks.

Step 4: How much ownership and interaction will be required among participants?

- Make sure that it is not pseudo-involvement but real and valuable involvement. To get the output that you defined in step 2, what is really needed from participants to get to that end result? This will set up the requirements for step 5.

Step 5: What platform and software does it require?

- As a rule of thumb, the technology should always follow the workshop's purpose. There are meeting platforms (e.g. Zoom, MS Teams, Skype, WebEx, GoToMeeting) that you will need to speak and interact, and there are collaboration platforms (e.g. Mural, Miro, Klaxoon) to ideate and build solutions together live. In addition, you can find communication platforms that are helpful in preparing or hosting in-between activities (such as SharePoint, Howspace, Gnowbe, CrowdLab, Nosco, MS Planner).

Step 6: How will you do project management around the event?

- Who will be project leader, and what team will be organising all the details?
- How will you ensure production and facilitation of the event?
- What resources do you already have in-house, and where would you benefit from external assistance and consulting?

During a virtual large-scale event

When you're running a virtual large-scale event, you want to be there at least an hour before it is due to start – to make sure that your tech setup is right and that you have the opportunity to arrive in the room, prepare yourself, get your notes out and check that you have everything you need at hand.

We recommend that one of your assistants logs into the session 15 minutes before it is due to start. Make sure that you have your music on and that the virtual space is set up as you want it. Once you start delivering the session, you can't deviate too much from the playbook. In fact, it's almost like you're pressing play on a pre-recorded session, because you want to run your playbook as planned. As the lead facilitator, you need to be aware of the many roles people will be playing around you. You'll have someone on the production setup, maybe someone else who handles the chat function, maybe a camera operator and maybe a co-facilitator. Then you will have the subject matter expert(s) and/or leader(s) who will be joining at various points. There will be lots of different partners in play and you need to produce and handle them.

As a result, your playbook should be much more detailed than it would be for a smaller session, down to the timing of the slide changes in your presentations. Make sure that your playbook has been shared with the team around you and that you have walked through it before the session. Everybody should map out what their role is at each point in time throughout the session.

> *Top tip: Sit down with your whole team before the session to walk through the playbook and encourage everyone to make notes about roles, where they should be when, what they should do, what their cue is for X, Y, Z, and so on.*

You'll want to make the delivery of the session as professional as possible. For virtual large-scale events you'll be broadcasting from a studio, so make sure that your team isn't talking in the background to keep it professional. Agree beforehand on how you will communicate when you are live, so that everyone is familiar with any non-verbal signals you'll be giving.

> *Top tip: Have a clear agreement within your team about how you communicate. It could be something simple like agreeing on a sign for changing slides. You*

should also have a sign to indicate that you need help with something. It's important to know how you can help one another and have those discussions if you actually need to handle something during a session.

When you are presenting, we recommend that you stand up instead of sitting down. This creates more energy and you also talk more freely when you are standing than when you are sitting. Talk directly to the camera. Usually, when you get to the stage that you are delivering these kinds of events, you'll be using a dedicated full HD webcam or a professional camera. Those are usually positioned pretty high and can therefore be at eye level.

Top tip: One thing we have found is that people often find it hard to be engaging when they're talking straight to a camera. If you can, get someone to stand directly behind the camera so that you can talk to them. This can make the setup feel more human and that will help you deliver a more engaging presentation.

We would also recommend using an external mic so that you aren't restricted by a headset. Position the mic in front of you but out of the camera shot. This will give you the freedom to move around while you talk. Another option is to have a mic with wireless transmission that you clip onto your clothes. It's good to include physical movement if possible, because this introduces some variation to the session. Even something as simple as moving back from the camera to point at something, or to write on a flip chart, can help create some good energy, which is picked up by the camera and filters out to the participants.

You could also explore having your presentation mounted on a wall, rather than just using slides, and having a camera operator following you as you point to different things. This kind of variation is really nice for the presenter, as well as making the session more interesting and engaging for the audience.

Don't be afraid to get your participants physically moving. You can get them to do all kinds of things, from planks to sit-ups. If you are going to do these kind of energiser exercises, like the ones we suggested in Chapter 10, then you need to go into them with all your energy and belief, and you'll find that everyone else follows. Bring your co-host to support you on screen, if you have one.

> *Top tip: Rather than getting a senior executive or a leader to deliver a presentation with a big slide-show, interview them and share the information in this format instead. Consider also introducing the option of the participants asking questions for the person being interviewed, either through the chat or in breakouts. If you choose to do this, make sure you have a person whose role is to check the chat, filter the questions and feed the relevant ones to the facilitator who is conducting the interview. This is a great way of engaging the entire crowd and making that element of your session more energetic, as well as more meaningful and relevant to the participants. This also allows the person being interviewed to come across as more passionate and authentic than if they were just to deliver a PowerPoint presentation.*

If you want to use breakouts, assign people to breakouts in an easy way and make sure that it's simple for them to enter the breakout room and return to the main session. In Zoom, for instance, it's very easy to do and it's a smooth journey for the user. It comes back to the idea of thinking about your participants' digital maturity and what they are used to. You should always choose the most frictionless option.

> *Top tip: Be aware that preassigned groups with more than 50 participants can be a nightmare to handle depending on the software. If this is the case, make sure it's doable.*

After a virtual large-scale event

What you need to be especially aware of after a virtual large-scale event is the follow-up, and there are two tempos you can use. The first is the fast follow-up. This should be sent shortly after the session. It is usually an email along the lines of, 'Thank you for a really inspiring session. . .' and then you share the slides or some highlights. What you need to remember is that normally these large-scale sessions are about launching a change, a new strategy or something that you want people to continue talking about afterwards.

Within a couple of days to a week after the session, you should send your second follow-up. A video is nice for this one, but what you are looking for is a way of condensing the input that you got from the session and sharing some key takeaways with the participants. It's very important that you follow up with something afterwards for two reasons. The first is to show them that the input they provided has made a difference, and the second is to encourage them to keep talking about it.

Top tip: A follow-up activity we strongly recommend after a virtual large-scale event is to continue with local activities. These could be physical or virtual. The idea behind them is that they translate this big communication into a local sense-making session, where you explain what it means for each team or department. This kind of follow-up should be part of your process design. You'll need to send out a small kit to the local managers to enable them to host these sessions, either virtually or physically, where they discuss and translate what was shared in your virtual large-scale event. Also consider whether you need to train the local managers to host those sessions, but again that falls under the planning phase.

It's essential to get feedback from virtual large-scale events and evaluate the learnings you can take from them. It's important because you spend so long on the planning phase, you need to know whether everything has gone as planned. You need to learn from this for future virtual large-scale events.

We also recommend getting feedback from the participants to find out how your session was received. Normally you would ask for this kind of feedback using a survey form, either as part of the end of the session or in the follow-up. Make sure the feedback format provides you with some learnings and guidance to help you in the planning and delivery of your next virtual large-scale event. Remember it is a huge investment of time both for the participants and the planning team, so you want to ensure maximum impact and learning out of this and any future large-scale sessions.

Case: Virtual HR leadership summit

A two-day summit for the 50 top leaders within HR. Normally people will fly from around the world to attend this annual summit. The global strategy for the organisation has just been launched, but now this must be translated into an HR-specific context to create ownership around it. There have been almost no similar high-profile events for senior leaders to get inspiration from, and the impression in the organisation is that hosting a two-day virtual summit will be a boring one-way session.

Purpose	The purpose of the summit is threefold:
	• Mobilise the HR Leadership team to help increase HR's impact, brand and shared voice as a function.
	• Create understanding and buy-in to HR strategy and clear line of sight to corporate strategy and business strategies.
	• Set clear expectations to HR leaders to be driving the ambitions in their own teams.
Success criteria	• Increase collaboration among HR leaders.
	• Gain multiple ideas on how to challenge the business on the themes within the strategy.
	• Make time to have meaningful and deep conversations with other HR leaders about the strategy.
	• Provide time for questions, and get answers from administration about the strategy.

Participants	50 HR leaders who are part of the leadership team
	6 Participants from the global leadership team
	2 Executive vice presidents
	1 External speaker
	1 Facilitator / Moderator
	1 Technical assistant
	2 Project team / Personal assistants
Platform	Zoom – as video conference tool
	Office 360 PowerPoint Shared documents – for capturing the breakout discussions
	MentiMeter – for quick polls, quizzes and feedback
	1 control room on the day, 1 conference room for the executive vice presidents
Process	2 days with a four-hour session on each
	Combination of plenary sessions and breakout rooms
	Documenting inputs in shared documents
Partners	Facilitator: Handling all the transitions, setting up the activities
	EVP: Setting the context for each part, presenting content of the strategy, debriefing output on activities, listening in and being available for questions in breakout and in plenary

The participants were invited to a two-day workshop, where they were to have meaningful dialogues among the leaders, to create a common understanding of the new global strategy.

We decided to split the summit into two four-hour sessions to ensure full focus from participants.

We switched between the executive vice president presenting the strategy and giving the participants time to discuss in breakout sessions of 3–4 people. Here they discussed how to realise the strategy in their team. They documented the conversations in a shared document where questions and blank fields for making notes guided their conversations. Also we included elements with Q&A with the executive management team and presented the leading research on the topic.

During the breakout sessions, the executive vice president visited all breakout rooms, to be available for further explanations and curious about their reflections. Returning from the breakout rooms to plenary, there was an opportunity to share conclusions and ask questions to EVP and the other teams.

Throughout the agenda we created energy and connection as a group through virtual energisers, where participants did small workouts or fun quizzes.

The days ended with an evaluation of the summit and by sharing personal highlights.

The days ended with an evaluating of

'Worked extremely well:) Nice seeing so many colleagues using the camera as well....'

'Thank you for an amazing 2 days. Stay safe and be well!'

'It was also extremely well organised by Implement – you did a phenomenal job'

Special takeaways from this case

- Let the participants spend 50% of the time in breakout, if the purpose is to create ownership and networking.

- When there are many people joining, and the session is important, spend a lot of time on preparation, to align on format, content, preparation, participants and also ensure all stakeholders know what to do on the day.

(We spend 3 weeks planning this session, with a total of 10 full days planning the session.)

- Have a dedicated facilitator running the day with help from a technical assistant and a project manager working behind the scenes.

28

The Final Word

Our reason for writing this book is to inspire people all around the world to have better virtual sessions. We see a great potential out there – to have more virtual sessions to take care of our planet, be efficient and create flexible working conditions. And we also see a huge demand among our colleagues and clients to learn *how* virtual sessions can be facilitated with energy and engagement to ensure high quality virtual sessions. As we wrote in the beginning – virtual facilitation is a twenty-first century skill to build for you as a virtual facilitator and a capability of any modern organisation.

Throughout this book we have tried our best to share our extensive knowledge about best practice when facilitating virtual sessions such as meetings, workshops and training. Experience based on years of practice, both in traditional and virtual sessions. To give an idea of the amount of experience we have brought to you from Implement Consulting Group, we built upon more than 4,000 Zoom sessions and 160+ webinars and trained more than 7,000 people just within the first half of 2020.

Going through the basic elements of virtual facilitation, the entire process – before, during and after – and paying further attention to the various formats, we hope you are inspired. Both by a high-level structural approach to virtual sessions alongside lots of small tips and tricks to refine the sessions. We hope you won't wait for 'someone' to do 'something'. Start with your own meetings, workshops or training and it will gradually change your organisation.

Take advantage of the online community

Acknowledging that virtual facilitation is a moving target we created an online community. If you haven't already done so, we encourage you to take a look once in a while to stay updated. We will keep you abreast of the latest news and you can also find the materials, templates and further inspiration for the book here. Go check it out.

We can all learn something new

When we look at facilitators – whether you are all new to it or you have many years of experience – we can all learn something new. We believe that anyone can learn virtual facilitation. Writing this book made it even more evident to us how many instruments and tricks – both large and small – a facilitator can use to increase the quality of the session, creating clarity, engagement and reaching the purpose with the participants. We encourage all facilitators to take upon themselves the challenge of continuous improvement.

Our hope is that you will use this book to be curious and challenge yourself. To look at your virtual session, take what you read and put it into practice. Virtual sessions do not have to be all about PowerPoints and one-way communication. Try something new – dare to engage your audience.

Start small – continue to build your skills

Our best advice is to get started right away. We do not expect you to take everything from this book and implement it right away. Actually, our suggestion is not to. We know from many years of experience that trying to do everything at once is very difficult – it's likely to fail and you'll end up demotivated.

We suggest that you start with one thing, one focus area. If you have made a list, or bookmarked pages with Post-it notes, briefly go through these. Look at them and select one that you are most curious about trying out, or maybe something that you think will have the biggest impact on the purpose of your session. Whether this is using the Design Star for planning, adding breakout rooms or something completely different is up to you.

If you don't know where to begin, we recommend starting with the purpose of your session, right in the middle of the Design Star. Define it, discuss it with your planning team or other relevant stakeholders. Make sure you're fluent with it. Read more about how to do this in Chapter 6 and Chapter 7.

Look at yourself and your current skills and challenge yourself from there. Work with this one element and figure out how it alters your sessions, your participants, and the effect it has. See how you can add value this way. Master it.

Remember to get feedback – from yourself, your participants and your stakeholders. You might even record the session to review yourself on screen (yes, it can feel intimidating and, yet, it is one of the most efficient ways to become a better facilitator as you see how you come across onscreen!)

During this process you will learn to master this element – a new skill that will become natural during your sessions. You no longer have to spend a lot of energy doing this – it will be a natural part of your skillset. As you reach this point of mastery you are ready to move on to the next element. This is when you can go back to your list, if you have it, and pick what you'd like to work on as a next step.

You might want to reread the relevant parts in the book covering this element, maybe you need to revisit the book for further inspiration or maybe you should take a look at our community for the latest inspiration on virtual facilitation.

Imagine if you could be the one hosting the virtual meeting that people were truly looking forward to!

Good luck with your virtual sessions.

About the Authors

About Implement

How can organisations become truly fit for humans and fit for the future? More competitive, adaptable and sustainable – and more innovative, engaging and entrepreneurial?

We believe it calls for an uncompromising combination of deep functional and transformational expertise. It also calls for a certain mindset: that all change starts with people and that consulting is, in essence, helping. And it demands we work in small, agile teams committed to creating impact together with our clients.

Headquartered in Copenhagen with offices in Aarhus, Stockholm, Malmo, Oslo, Zurich and Munich, we are fortunate to count more than 900 colleagues working globally with clients on projects of all shapes, sizes and ambitions.

***

Henrik has written a number of articles on the topic of change management and facilitation and co-authored *Facilitation – Create Results Through Involvement*. As an advisor to major multinationals, Henrik has extensive experience facilitating large-scale c-suite seminars and training events, often as centrepieces of new strategy or company-wide change programme implementation.

A board member of Implement Consulting Group and chairman of the board of the Danish Association of Management Consulting Companies, Henrik is dedicated to helping the consulting industry become more collaborative, impactful and human.

***

Kåre is a virtual facilitation nerd, with deep subject matter expertise helping both Implement and its clients accelerate their virtual transformations. Having trained thousands in the field of virtual facilitation, Kåre's practical experience extends to enabling global industry leaders to expand their virtual capabilities.

With a background within education and positive psychology, Kåre believes that virtual facilitation needs to combine the technical possibilities with knowledge about human psychology to ensure motivation and to create results together.

***

Iben is a learning expert, specialising in accelerated learning within onboarding, leadership training and workshop facilitation. She works a lot with the design and execution of meetings, onboarding and leadership programmes. Iben also conducts train-the-trainer programmes both for her colleagues at Implement as well as clients. Her toolbox includes brain-friendly principles, practical training and a strong focus on engagement as keys to facilitate the learning process. With a master's degree in political science and a background in sports and physical science, Iben excels at helping clients and colleagues combine clever insights with practical knowledge and training to create real impact for individuals, teams and organisations.

***

The insights and ideas presented in this book come from years of working hands-on with facilitation, literally experiencing what works and what doesn't, what's easy and what's not, as it happens. We hope you will be inspired to run even better virtual sessions with more engagement and impact.

Acknowledgements

The book you are holding in your hands is the result of many years of experience with facilitation – physical and virtual. We, as authors, have done our best to gather all we know about the topic and provide it for you to use to become a better virtual facilitator. Yet to do this we have been helped, inspired and challenged by colleagues and clients around us.

Brave and courageous consulting colleagues, both current and former, have shared their ideas and learnings within the topic or even brought us to their sessions to see and learn for ourselves.

We feel honoured to be a part of an organisation where experiments, and the courage to try new things in order to humanise the virtual space, are a part of our culture. We have used our experience as a resource of practical knowledge – on what to do, and what not to do. Hopefully, with this book, we have succeeded in gathering all the important 'dos' and presenting them in ways that you can use – and even to take them further.

Through a series of more than 50 webinars in only 4 months, our marketing department, together with great consultants, have demonstrated how the corona crisis can be used to develop a new format to inspire clients with our core ideas. Learnings from these webinars also play a key role in this book. Actually, the entire brand service department also deserves a huge acknowledgement for

327

their help with the book, the online repository and for always being helpful and delivering high quality in any matter.

A special thanks to Cecilie Van Loon and Line Larsen. Together with Henrik they wrote the book *Facilitation – Create Results Through Involvement*, published in 2017. All the valuable discussions, hard work and tools in that book have defined the mindset upon which this book on virtual facilitation builds.

Our clients have been a huge part of this journey. They are, with all their differences, a continuing source of inspiration. They keep challenging us to do more – do better – create more impact and be more human. They have trusted us, been courageous in their efforts, and supportive in our learning journey, as we explore this new land in the quest to create more engaging virtual meetings.

This book was written over the summer of 2020. Our families have supported us during the process, accepting shortened summer holidays, late evenings by the computer or virtual Teams meetings across three cabins and, in essence, coping with us and our passion for what we do. We are deeply thankful for your continuous support and for being who you are!

Index